The People

Books by Pat Anderson

NOVELS
The McGlinchy Code
The Crimes of Miss Jane Goldie
Torrent
A Toast to Charlie Hanrahan
Catalyst

FACTUAL
Clash of the Agnivores
Never Mind the Zombies
Rattus Agnivoricus
Damned Agnivores
Another Zombie in a Different Kitchen
Fear and Smear
Yellow Peril
Up to Our Knees
The Boattum Line (by Billy 'Burger' King)

FOR CHILDREN
The Skyscraper Rocket Ship
The Ceremony at Goreb Ridge
The Brain Thing
The Football Star
Mighty Pete and the
School Bully School

The People

A SHORT HISTORY OF THE BAND THAT TIME FORGOT

Pat Anderson

Snowy Publications MMXVIII

Copyright © 2018 Pat Anderson
All rights reserved.

ISBN: 9781791732622

Here's to Ten in a Row!

Contents

Preface ix

Introduction... xi

1. Starting Over 1
2. Heaven Is A Place On Earth................... 16
3. Let's Work Together 27
4. People Get Ready 42
5. Church Of The Poison Mind 49
6. You Put Your Right Leg In 60
7. Walk This Way... 67
8. Culture Shock 75
9. Boys Keep Swinging............................... 85
10. I Can Sing A Rainbow 96
11. Your Own Personal Jesus 106
12. If You're Irish Come Into The Parlour ... 120
13. With A Little Help From My Friends 131
14. Que Sera Sera....................................... 142
Notes 149

Preface

I decided to write this book while taking a break from writing the follow-up to A *Toast to Charlie Hanrahan*. I was getting a bit stuck, trying to think what was going to happen next so I moved on to something a bit more straightforward for a while. The story of The People practically wrote itself; all the material was already there. Hopefully, you enjoy reading it as much as I enjoyed writing it.

You will notice that I have left out one of the great obsessions of The People; the sexual abuse of children. I did this because I wanted the book to be entertaining as well as (hopefully) informative. There is nothing entertaining about using sexual abuse to score points and it was something I would rather not go into. We should just assume that it is simply part-and-parcel of The People's mentality. If we understand something of their psyche, then we can, perhaps, understand why they will use any means to attack their imagined enemies.

Apologies for the state of some of the endnotes I have tried my best to fix them and make them look tidy, but to no avail. Maybe someday I will figure it out!

So, anyway, here it is. I do not pretend that it is an exhaustive study, but I hope to have provided some insights into the crazy world of The People.

Read my blog here:
https://paddyontherailway.wordpress.com/

Follow me on Twitter: @PatAndersptr

Introduction

We have all heard the cry, 'We are The People' and have struggled to know what it means. Mind you, The People themselves have no idea what it means and can never explain when anyone asks. The stock answer betrays this ignorance: 'To those that understand, no explanation is necessary. To those that do not, no explanation is possible.' Simply put, this is a verbose way of saying, 'I don't know.' It is something, though, that they refuse to admit.

There have been many histories written about Rangers and the main characters involved in it. Hagiographies of Bill Struth are ten a penny as are all the stories about 'Four men' having a dream. It is made to look like a great struggle against adversity; a football version of *Rocky*. The supporters, The People, honestly believe this hokum and have the view that the whole world was against Rangers from its inception right up to its demise.

Since the death of Rangers, The People have had their work cut out trying to keep up the pretence that the new club is still the old club. Of course, they have been helped in this fallacy by the Scottish football authorities and the Scottish media. Not that they are in the least grateful; they actually complain that the SFA, the SPFL and the media in Scotland have it in for them.

Strangely, nobody has ever written the story of The People, even though they are a fascinating study. Anyone that has tackled this type of history has always done so by looking at the supporters of the 'Old Firm'. Nobody seems to want to separate them, viewing them as 'just as bad as each other'. This, however, is completely untrue and the differences between the two sets of supporters has been brought into sharp focus with the death of Rangers and the consequent disappearance of the Old Firm.

There are supporters of football teams all over the world that can be characterised as arrogant, but none of them even come close to The People. Their new club, which they argue is still the old club, is, apparently, the 'most successful football club in the world'. Certainly, Rangers held the record, and still do, for the most domestic league titles.[1] It is arguable, though, whether that makes them even Britain's most successful club, never mind the world's.

They have never won the European Cup and only have one European Cup Winners Cup to their name; won, it has to be said, in rather dodgy circumstances.

Nobody can tell The People that, though. And it does not matter that leagues in other countries are much harder to win; all they look at is the number 54. More than a few of those 54 should not count at all since Rangers cheated to achieve them. Again, however, The People will not hear of such a thing and threaten violence to anyone in authority that dares to suggest that those league titles should be removed. Not that they need to resort to violence, since they have the football authorities and all the Scottish media on their side.

But The People do not stop at exaggerating the achievements of their dead club. The way they go on it is as if Rangers, and the new club, Neo-Gers, have operated and do operate under royal appointment. They call their team the 'Queen's 11', as if Auld Lizzie takes great interest in the club. If she ever has paid any attention to them it was probably in anger at losing out on her share of the taxes that Rangers refused to pay. But, still, they portray themselves as the Queen's most loyal subjects and believe that she reciprocates that love and devotion.

They go even further than that, though. They think that their team has been blessed by God and that they are the Almighty's Chosen People. (Hence their self-given name.) Since they have this belief, it is perhaps understandable that they think they are superior to everyone else and have an arrogant sense of entitlement. After all, if God's Chosen are not entitled to success, then who is?

As well as their arrogance and misplaced sense of superiority, The People are also renowned for their lack of brain cells. This, of course, begs the question of where they got all their ideas from; how did they come up with the notion that they are God's Chosen People and are better than everyone else? It hardly seems likely that they sit around discussing theology and soteriology. The simple answer is that they did not come up with these ideas; someone else did.

To understand the way The People think, it is necessary to go back about 600 years. Let us start at the very beginning. As Julie Andrews pointed out, it is a very good place to start.

The People

e.

1
Starting Over

Ask anybody these days what the Reformation was about, and they'll tell you it happened because of all the corruption in the Catholic Church. Unfortunately, back then, there was plenty to complain about. Priests were shacked up with concubines, while their bishops were often unaware of what was going on since they were too busy raking in the cash from the multiple posts they held. Even popes were known to have mistresses and offspring, whom they unashamedly promoted to positions of power.

Then there was the relics industry. Throughout Europe, there were probably enough pieces of the True Cross to build a battleship, while the bones of saints could fetch a fortune. Kings, princes and bishops would pay handsomely for a bone belonging to a saint. Again, there were so many bones around that folk must have believed all the saints to have been giants and, without proper tests available, nobody really knew what they were buying. In many cases the bones were probably only fit to be handed to a dog.

So fierce was the competition for these relics that folk would resort to any trick to get one. I remember reading the story of one bishop, desperate for a decent relic for his cathedral. He made the journey to a church that had the bone of a saint on display. He knelt and kissed the bone to show his devotion and, when he was sure nobody was looking, he bit a chunk off to take home with him!

The best relics were those that were connected with Jesus and his mother, Mary. Unfortunately, both of them had ascended into Heaven without leaving so much as a bone behind. A lot of ingenuity was applied in this respect. Since Jesus was a Jew, he had obviously lost one piece of his body and there were scores of Holy Foreskins to be found all over Europe. There were also samples of Mary's breast milk; a relic that could, more credibly, exist in multiples. I have never seen mention of a Holy Afterbirth but, no doubt, some enterprising church somewhere would have had one.

Pilgrimages to these shrines was big business and one could book the equivalent of a package holiday, visiting various relics, with transport and accommodation included. No doubt pilgrims had a great time on their travels but that was not the point of the trip. The main reason for visiting these shrines was to earn an *indulgence*; which granted you time off in Purgatory.

Only the perfectly good got straight into Heaven and only the perfectly evil went straight to Hell. Most people were somewhere in between these two extremities and so were sent to another place altogether. It stood to reason that a loving God would not want to throw His children into Hell for comparatively minor sins, so theologians came up with the idea of Purgatory. There, you would suffer for your sins for a finite period and then be allowed into Heaven.

Life was viewed as a balance-sheet, with all the good you had done being on the credit side, while your sins made up the debit column. How much debit you had would determine how long you would have to spend in Purgatory. There were ways, however, that you could get time knocked off.

Doing good was an obvious way, but one could also benefit from Grace. Grace was God's gift to the penitent, through the Church. Jesus's sacrifice on the cross was the main source of Grace, and one could be forgiven, and receive Grace, by confessing one's sins to a priest or a friar. You had to be in what was called 'a state of Grace' to receive the Eucharist, which also imparted God's Grace. If you were truly penitent, then going to Confession wiped the slate clean and you got to start over.

As well as God's Grace, the exceptional goodness of the saints had built up a surplus, which could be drawn upon by the Church. Jesus had said to St. Peter:

> And I will give unto thee the keys of the kingdom of heaven: and whatsoever thou shalt bind on earth shall be bound in heaven: and whatsoever thou shalt loose on earth shall be loosed in heaven.[1]

The Pope was St. Peter's successor, so he had the keys and he, and the Church, were entitled to use them as they wished. Having the keys of Heaven implied that the Pope also had the keys to Purgatory. He, and the Church, were able, then, to offer people reduced time in

Purgatory by means of indulgences. Pilgrimages were a way of gaining indulgences, with set amounts of time off for visiting different shrines; the more important the shrine, the more time you got off.

Even when you died you could still ensure that you got a reduced sentence in Purgatory; especially if you were well-off. Poorer people might pray for the souls of friends and family, but the rich could leave behind money so that Masses could be offered up. If you were really wealthy, you could endow a whole building with clerics, called a college, where Masses would be said in perpetuity for your soul.

Other, more minor ways, to make sure that prayers were said on your behalf were leaving money for a bridge, a seat or a stained-glass window. As long as your name was on it, people would know who gifted it and who to pray for. At the very least, one should at least have a headstone on one's grave in the churchyard. Every prayer counted.

There was one aspect of indulgences, however, that not everyone agreed with; their sale. It was a quick and easy way for the Church to raise money for specific projects, like rebuilding St. Peter's Basilica in the Vatican. This could be viewed as people donating money to the Church and receiving an indulgence in return, or as a serious abuse of the Church's spiritual power.

Since Martin Luther nailed his Ninety-Five Theses to the church door in Wittenberg in 1517, at the height of the raising of money for rebuilding St. Peter's, it is often thought that it was the sale of indulgences that he was arguing against.[2] If this had been the case, then he would not have to have left the Catholic Church and the Reformation would never have happened. After all, there were plenty of others arguing against the practice.

Against all the abuses in the Church were those writers known as Humanists. This 'Humanism' had nothing to do with the modern version, which tends to be atheistic and anti-religion. To distinguish it from modern Humanism, it is now called *Renaissance* Humanism.

When you mention the Renaissance, everyone invariably thinks of paintings, sculptures and the like. Of course, this was an essential part of the movement, with art, inspired by Classical statues, architecture etc., aiming for a new realism. A prime example of this is Jan van Eyck's *Arnolfini Portrait*,[3] where even the reflection in the mirror is rendered faithfully. But there was far more to it than that.

It is hard to pinpoint exactly when the Renaissance started but it was certainly in evidence from the end of the Fourteenth Century onwards. It was a craze for all things Roman and Greek; not only in the visual arts but in philosophy, public speaking, government and, of course, scripture. Everything was being looked at with new eyes and the excitement was palpable when, in 1453, Constantinople fell to the Ottomans and Greek refugees fled, bringing with them works of literature that had not been seen in western Europe for centuries.

Looking at Renaissance art reveals one of the prime elements of the movement: the elevation of man. Mankind was God's greatest creation and He had given humans intelligence, the ability to reason and free will.[4] Why would God give mankind such gifts if He did not intend them to use them? And did God not create man in His own image and likeness? Although Shakespeare was being ironic, his description in *Hamlet* nevertheless sums up Renaissance attitudes:

> What a piece of worke is a man! how Noble in Reason? how infinite in faculty? in forme and moving how expresse and admirable? in Action, how like an Angel? in apprehension how like a God?[5]

While artists were portraying the physical magnificence of God's greatest creation, Humanist writers concerned themselves with the mental and spiritual sides. This is often portrayed as a great enterprise of individualism and the embracing of social and religious freedom.[6] One had to be careful, however, not to overstate what the Renaissance Humanists achieved, or even wanted to achieve.

Nowadays, we are used to going to art galleries to see famous paintings. Even if we are unable to venture further afield, books and the internet let us see anything we want to. In Renaissance times, however, it has to be remembered that most art was commissioned by rich people and was hidden away in their own, private collections. It was rare for ordinary people to get a glimpse of Renaissance art, unless they were fortunate enough for an example to be available in their local church.

It was the same with literature. Only the wealthy could afford books, even when the advent of printing made them cheaper. Besides, most educated people wrote in Latin, which cut down the audience considerably. This is an important point; something that needs to be borne in mind throughout our look at Renaissance times and afterwards. Ordinary people did not have access to the outpouring of literature of those days.

Among the Renaissance Humanist writers, the most famous by far was, and is, Desiderius Erasmus (the son of a priest!), also known as Erasmus of Rotterdam. Other writers were well known to the educated throughout Europe, but Erasmus was a celebrity, known to everybody. Even ordinary people knew who he was, and Erasmus was not above basking in his celebrity and using it to his own advantage.

Towns, cities, universities, princes and kings all vied with each other to entice Erasmus to come and stay with them. They could then boast about their prize asset. A modern equivalent to this was when Madonna married Guy Ritchie and lived in England. The UK media went into overdrive with their claims that Madonna was 'theirs'; they even called her 'Madge'.

Erasmus was an inveterate traveller and was happy to take up some of these offers, even teaching at Queens College, Cambridge for a time. Eventually, though, he decided that he wanted to concentrate on his writing. All he wanted from life was paper and pen for his books, translations and copious correspondence, convivial company, a comfortable billet, decent food and somebody to pay for it all. Fortunately, his celebrity status meant he rarely had to put his hand in his own pocket.

Like other Humanists, Erasmus was critical of abuses in the Church, which he parodied to great effect in his book, *In Praise of Folly*. He also laid great emphasis on spirituality, saying that it was more important than physical manifestations. He was keen too on education and was in favour of laypeople reading the scriptures. These views were to come back to haunt him in later years.

In Praise of Folly was a prime example of what was discussed earlier; literature was the preserve of the elite. The work was written in Latin, with the title *Moriae Encomium*. The word *moria* (μωρια) meant *folly* in Ancient Greek, but it was also a pun on the name of Erasmus's good friend Thomas More. Only the well educated would understand this, which shows the intended audience of the piece. (It also shows how easily pleased they were in those days when it came to humour!)

The message of the Renaissance Humanists was not for the common herd. Yes, they might argue for universal education and for the laity to have access to the scriptures, but it was understood that this did not apply to the likes of peasants and common workers. Erasmus's *New Testament*, for example, was written in Latin and Greek; it was obviously not intended for perusal by common eyes.

The point of highlighting Erasmus and the Renaissance Humanists is that if Luther was simply concerned about corruption in the Catholic Church, he was in good company. The likes of Erasmus and his English friend Thomas More, however, saw no need to leave the Catholic Church. All that was needed was for the corruption to be swept away and everything would be fine. Obviously, Luther's arguments went much deeper than looking to abolish the sale of indulgences and the like.

Luther was not just against the sale of indulgences; he was against the whole concept of indulgences altogether. In fact, he went further than that: there was no need for indulgences at all since Purgatory did not exist. This was not just an attack on corruption in the Church; it was a full-scale assault on the Church's soteriology, how it viewed people's salvation. It was this that caused all the trouble and sparked the Reformation.

Others were later to claim to have come to the same conclusions independently, but nobody could deny that Martin Luther was the first to publicly declare his discovery. What Luther suggested was revolutionary. There was no need to constantly fret about sinning and striving to be good; all one needed was faith. If you had faith in Christ, then that was it; you were saved. *Justification by Faith*, it was called.

This was a liberating message and Luther certainly expressed it as such. It was not a new interpretation of the scriptures; St. Augustine had reached the same conclusions away back in the early Fifth Century.[7] His explanation about the Fall of Man, Original Sin, had been kept by the Church, but it was argued that this inherited stain on the human soul was cleansed by the sacrament of Baptism. Luther, however, begged to differ.

As an Augustinian monk, Luther was obviously familiar with the man after whom his order was named. Humanist writers had also produced new translations and new commentaries on

Augustine's work, to which Luther obviously had access. What Augustine had to say about the human condition, however, would have made a Humanist's blood run cold.

After the Fall, Augustine argued, man was a debased creature, about as far from God as it was possible to get. There was no way that such a miserable specimen as man could contribute to his own salvation, the way that Pelagius, Augustine's contemporary, argued.[8] He was totally reliant upon the good will of God. Only God could save man from his wretchedness; there was nothing at all that man could do.

To Luther, the Catholic Church had moved away from the beliefs of its early Fathers. It was as if Pelagius had won and Augustine tossed aside. Only through God's Grace could man be saved. Although this meant that man could not do anything to help his own salvation, it also meant that man *did not have to* do anything for his salvation. It was an attractive prospect. Unfortunately, the adage that if a deal sounds too good to be true, it usually is, was applicable to this soteriology. There was a catch; a huge one.

Augustine's opinions can appear contradictory to the modern eye,[9] supporting predestination one minute and free will the next. His writings show that, in his mind, he was attempting a balancing act between two extremes and the Catholic Church had followed him in this. Essentially, what the Catholic Church said was that, although God has foreknowledge of what we are going to do, He does not force us to do it; we make the choice of our own free will whether to do good or to sin.

This is an extremely difficult balance to maintain. If the Church had tipped the scales in favour of free will, it was hardly surprising; the Gospels, after all, claimed that Christ came to save *everybody*. In his more extreme moments, when he was arguing against Pelagius, Augustine appeared to take the complete opposite view. It was this view that Luther took to be the truth.

From reading St. Paul's Epistles, Augustine, and Luther after him, interpreted certain passages to mean that God had already chosen who was going to be saved before time began. God is a perfect being and, as such, cannot change His mind since this would imply that He had been in error and was therefore imperfect. Since He could foresee who would choose to follow the Christian message and who would not, even before He had made them, then He made people knowing who would go to Heaven and who would not. Since mankind could only be saved through God's Grace, God chose to whom he would impart Grace. These fortunate souls were called 'The Elect'.

This was, and is, a rather frightening prospect, but there it is, in black and white, not only in Augustine's writings but in those of St. Paul as well.[10] And, if we are to take scripture as the arbiter of everything religious, then we cannot ignore these passages just because it suits us. It is noticeable, however, that the idea of predestination and 'The Elect' does not feature in the Gospels.

When I read the New Testament, admittedly quite some time ago, it struck me how different was the message imparted by Paul from that of Jesus in the Gospels. Jesus had announced a 'New Covenant', replacing the old one God had made with the Chosen People. This new covenant was for all of mankind; not just the Jews. You would never guess that, however, if you only read Paul's Epistles.

It is worth remembering that Paul was a Jewish fundamentalist before he was a Christian and he appeared to carry this fundamentalism over into his new religion. Most of the advice and admonition he sends to different churches in his Epistles tends to come from the Old Testament, rather than from Christ's teachings. For example, his hostility to women taking an active part in the Church comes straight from Jewish law, as Paul admits himself:

> Let your women keep silence in the churches: for it is not permitted unto them to speak; but they are commanded to be under obedience, as also saith the law.[11]

I was a teenager when I read the New Testament, but even then, Paul reminded me of some American Evangelical Preacher, speaking of God's love while ranting about the things he hates. He even seemed to have it in for hippies, demanding that, if you wanted to be a Christian, you should have a short-back-and-sides![12] As you might gather, I've never been much of a fan of St. Paul.

Be that as it may, Humanist writers, like Erasmus, now faced a dilemma. They were the ones that had advocated reading the Bible carefully and reaching your own conclusions. It was they that had churned out versions of Augustine's writings. Now they had spawned a movement that went against everything they stood for. Instead of man being God's greatest creation, he was less than worthless. And instead of man being able to figure things out for himself and choose to do the right thing, he was merely pre-programmed to behave in the way God made him.

Humanists might have criticised the Church and pointed out areas of corruption, but this was something different entirely. This was a challenge to Church doctrine, denying the soteriology of the Church. It was too much for some Humanists to accept; Sir Thomas More, the author of *Utopia*, chose the axeman's block rather than renounce his Catholic faith. Nobody would dare chop Erasmus's head off, but he found himself derided and ridiculed by both sides.

It is unknown who first came up with the phrase, 'Erasmus laid the egg that Luther hatched,' but it was both compliment and condemnation. Protestants still use the saying to show how their beliefs have their roots in Renaissance Humanism. Erasmus was none too happy about this observation, which suggests that it first came from Roman Catholics, blaming him for the Lutheran schism. Erasmus's answer was that 'Luther had hatched a different bird entirely.'[13] In point of fact, Erasmus, although trying to remain neutral in the doctrinal arguments, found himself in profound disagreement with Luther.

Erasmus, however, was howling at the wind with his writings about free will. Luther's ideas were taken up by others and were here to stay. Erasmus had to watch, impotent, as the Western Church fell apart. He might, though, have found some comfort in the fact that Luther did not have things all his own way.

Luther, and other Reformers, wanted to take the Church back to what it had been in Augustine's time. They had no problem with the Nicene Creed but argued that their view of salvation was what the Church should be about. They had not intended to break away from Roman Catholicism; but, in their view, *they* were the real, proper Catholics. They were not the only ones that could read the Bible, though, and others wanted to go further; much further.

Some folk noticed that in the Bible there was no mention anywhere of infant baptism. Surely original Christianity taught that one should be an adult and make a conscious choice to be baptised? There was also no mention in the Bible of trinities, Holy or otherwise and it appeared that original Christians shared all their possessions and did not believe in private property. There was no way that any royalty or nobility was going to accept that!

And even among the Reformers themselves there was disagreement. The Swiss Reformer Huldrych Zwingli saw the Eucharist as being symbolic, while Luther, despite denying transubstantiation, believed that Christ was present in the Communion bread. Other Reformers smashed up church statues; Luther did not see any harm in them. And while Luther venerated the Virgin Mary, there were those that argued that she had been merely a vessel, nothing more.

Amid all the turmoil, as you might expect, the barns came crawling out. There were various prophets, saying that the world was going to end soon and that the faithful should gather in whatever city the prophet chose. Others claimed to be the Messiah, returned to save the world from sin. Rather worryingly, these delusional individuals actually had followers.

While university-educated scholars like Luther and Zwingli argued the toss about the Eucharist, it is doubtful that the general population understood any of these nuanced debates. To many, it was just a case of going to Mass, receiving the Eucharist and then going home. If their priest were to suddenly tell them that the Eucharist was not *literally* the Body of Christ, but a symbol, who were they to argue? Free Will, Predestination, Good Works, Justification by Faith; they were just words. All they wanted was for somebody to tell them what to do so that, after they died, they could have a better life than the one they had now.

There was one thing, however, that practically all the labouring classes hated about the Church: The Tithe. A tenth of everything they earned or produced had to go to the Church; this was on top of taxes that they had to pay to local lords etc. When it looked like Luther was breaking away from the Church and he was churning out pamphlets, proclaiming 'Liberty' it was perhaps understandable if people took it the wrong way.

The so-called *Peasants War* saw an uprising throughout the lands of the Holy Roman Empire (modern-day Germany). As their demands made clear, they were inspired by the ideas of the Reformation.[14] Disappointingly, although they were supported by Zwingli, Luther was horrified at what he had let loose. He hurried to distance himself from the uprising, publishing *Against the Murderous and Robbing Hordes of the Peasants*.[15] This made clear that, at least in secular matters, he was on the side of authority.

One cannot help but wonder, however, if that authority, the princes, dukes and electors of the various states in German, understood what Luther was saying any more than the peasants did. The nobility then, as now, was not renowned for its intelligence. In fact, the acceptance of Luther's message by many of them was possibly just a massive *GIRFUY* to their Habsburg overlords!

As the Sixteenth Century progressed the turmoil diminished, and the various messiahs and prophets were rounded up and burned, beheaded, drowned or imprisoned, while the peasants were, just as violently, put back in their place. Luther died in 1546, leaving behind a legacy he would not have wanted. Not only had the Reformers broken with the Catholic Church, but they themselves had splintered and begun to solidify into separate churches.

Protestantism, as it came to be called, could not present any kind of united front in the face of Roman Catholic hostility. The compromise of *cuius regio, eius religio* (the ruler decides the religion) provided a kind of *modus vivendi* in Europe, but tensions still remained. It did not take much for violence, or all-out war, to flare up.

But, let us leave this troubled, splintered Europe and concentrate on what Protestants had in common. After all, the very fact that they called themselves 'Protestants' shows that they believed that there was more uniting them and their various churches than dividing them. Essentially, what distinguished a Protestant from a Roman Catholic was belief in Justification by Faith and the predestined salvation of the Elect.

Luther's soteriology was finessed by other Protestants, most notably by John Calvin. Instead of pussyfooting about, trying to explain the doctrine of predestination by means of God having foreknowledge of people's goodness, Calvin just came straight out and claimed that it was purely God's will that some would be saved, and some would not. Since only God's Grace could save man, then it was purely His choice about to whom He would impart it. God's foreknowledge of man's goodness implies that man had some input into his salvation. Calvin utterly rejected this. It was God's Grace that made men good and His choice was purely arbitrary and only known to Him.[16]

Unlike other Protestant thinkers and writers, Calvin did not shy from the logical conclusions of his thesis. He advocated the concept of *Double Predestination*; not only had God already determined who would be saved, He had also determined who would be damned. Free will was now totally out the window, so to speak. You were what God made you and there was nothing you could do about it!

Of course, the most important aspect of anybody's life in this system was how could you know if you were one of the Elect or not. The answer was to look within yourself for proofs of your 'electedness'. It is unimaginable that anyone would look into himself and decide,

> 'Well, I'm obviously not one of the Elect – I might as well go and get pissed every night, shag who I want, male or female, steal anything I want and stab anybody that looks at me the wrong way. I'm going to Hell anyway!'

Calvin's ideas on predestination, however, turned the whole thing on its head. One would imagine that once you realised that you were one of the Elect, then it was time to get down to the church and do good works. To Calvin, the opposite was true. The very fact that you went to church, did good works and partook of the Eucharist, *proved* that you were one of the Elect. Only the Elect were predestined to be good so, if you were good, then you were obviously one of the Elect.[17] That man looking into himself and finding that he was not one of the Elect, then, could easily prove to himself, and others, that he *was*, simply by doing what everybody else was doing.

Calvin also outlined another proof that a person was one of the Elect; an idea that would have far-reaching implications, especially in Scotland. According to one commentator:

> Calvin also seemed to obscurely suggest that the daily blessings received from the hand of God might rightly be perceived as an indication of election.[18]

In other words, doing well in life showed that God favoured you above others. This was a strange idea, especially since Christ Himself had pointed out how difficult it was for a rich man to get into

Heaven.[19] Wealth had always posed a problem for the Church and Protestants took great delight in pointing to rich bishops, cardinals etc. as a sign of the corruption endemic in Roman Catholicism. And yet, here was Calvin saying that your wealth proved that you were one of the Elect. Needless to say, this only applied to the *Protestant* rich.

In 1529, Erasmus wrote of the Reformers' church services:

> I have never entered their conventicles, but I have sometimes seen them returning from their sermons, the countenances of all of them displaying rage, and wonderful ferocity, as though they were animated by the evil spirit....[20]

This rage and outright hatred were evident among Protestants almost as soon as the Reformation started. The Pope was represented as the Antichrist and the Whore of Babylon from the Book of Revelation in pamphlets and books.[21] This vilification was like nothing ever seen before. Humanist writers, and critics that existed before the Renaissance, might parody or condemn corruption and abuses in the Church, but they had never attacked the Church itself. Equally, individual popes, like Alexander VI or Pius II might be the subjects of criticism, but nobody had attacked the *institution* of the papacy before.

It could be argued that this was part-and-parcel of the general persecutions that were taking place at the time. Catholics killed Protestants, Protestants killed Catholics, while Anabaptists and witches were fair game no matter which church was in charge of where they were. All of this persecution and slaughter, however, was done under the law. Heresy was illegal both to Catholics and Protestants, as many an Anabaptist and Unitarian found to their cost. The vitriolic hatred and vilification of the Catholic Church, however, was outside of this legal framework.

In another attack on Luther, Erasmus said,

> You stipulate that we should not ask for or accept anything but Holy Scripture, but you do it in such a way as to require that we permit you to be its sole interpreter, renouncing all others. Thus the victory will

be yours if we allow you to be not the steward but the lord of Holy Scripture.[22]

This essentially accuses Luther of the sin of pride; a common complaint levelled against Protestants, especially Calvin. So, we have early Protestants apparently guilty of the sins of pride and hatred. But there is a possibility that these sins, or any sins, are not considered as such within the terms of Protestant doctrine.

There is a problem in Philosophy and Theology called the *Omnipotence Paradox*. Although this is expressed in the singular, it is actually composed of a number of different paradoxes. The idea is that, logically, different definitions of God contradict each other. The version I saw at university said,

> God is omnipotent.
> God can only do good.
> This restricts God's power, so He cannot be omnipotent.

This was presented as a logical proof that God cannot possibly exist. This particular argument, however, can easily be refuted, since it hinges on the presupposition that there is some abstract concept of 'Good' that God must adhere to. If one were to suggest that 'Good' only describes anything that God does, it puts a completely different slant on the statement. This also rather handily fits with Protestant theology, which claims that God's will and actions are a mystery to us, but they are, necessarily, because they are associated with God, good.

And what about the Elect; could the same argument affect them? We have already seen that the Elect are compelled to do good because God made them that way. It is a short step from that assertion to claiming that anything the Elect do is good. After all, God made them to be good by His own definition; and who are we to question that? I have not seen this explicitly claimed anywhere, but it is a reasonable inference to declare that the Elect are incapable of sinning. Perhaps our introspective friend, whom we met earlier, could live a life of debauchery and *still* get into Heaven!

There is also another aspect of Protestantism, and more especially Calvinism, that feeds into the idea that Protestants are allowed to be angry and hateful. It all stems from the reliance of Protestant churches on the Old Testament for verification of their doctrines.

As we saw earlier, nowhere in the Bible does it mention infant baptism, yet Protestant leaders were determined to retain it. They could hardly say that it was Church tradition, could they? In fact, they had made such a fuss about relying only on scripture for doctrine that they had to trawl through their Bibles for something, anything, to support infant baptism.

Fortunately for them, they found it in Genesis:

> And ye shall circumcise the flesh of your foreskin; and it shall be a token of the covenant betwixt me and you. And he that is eight days old shall be circumcised among you, every man child in your generations, he that is born in the house, or bought with money of any stranger, which is not of thy seed.[23]

God had demanded that his covenant with Abraham and his descendants be sealed by a ceremony involving infants. Why should He not demand the same of His Elect? His covenant with the Jews was sealed by circumcision, but it had been made clear in the New Testament that the New Covenant should be sealed by baptism. The Old Covenant had been entered into during infanthood, so why should the New Covenant not be the same?

This was not the only delve into the Old Testament by Protestant leaders. It was an obvious connection to make, to see the Elect as the new equivalent of the Chosen People. Since the only parts of the Bible to talk about the Chosen People are in the Old Testament, that was where Protestant preachers tended to look when writing their sermons.

When you compare the God of the Old Testament with that of the New, you could be forgiven for thinking that they are about two different Gods. The God of the New Testament is a loving and caring one that exhorts mankind to be the same. Jehovah, on the other hand, comes across as a capricious monster, smiting folk left, right and centre. Loving thy neighbour rarely comes into it.

This was the Protestantism that came to Scotland in the second half of the Sixteenth Century, dominated by John Knox, a keen follower of Calvin. It was a religion that was already tied to Old Testament ideas of a Chosen People, beset by enemies, and dedicated to a paranoid defence of its doctrines.

2
Heaven Is A Place on Earth

Life in Scotland in the Sixteenth Century sounds like a real barrel of laughs. It was a masochist's paradise. William Andrews outlined some of the punishments meted out, including the 'jougs' and the scold's bridle.[1] If you read his account you cannot fail to notice that most of these vicious devices were used on women. St. Paul would have been proud of them!

Actually, that statement about women needs qualification; most of Scotland's torture-chamber devices were used on *lower-class* women. Not only was the Church of Scotland a misogynist organisation, it also, apparently, discriminated against poor people.

Ordinary people lost the Feast Days that used to be celebrated under the old Church, including Christmas, which was even banned by law in 1640.[2] Dancing and drinking were frowned upon, as was any kind of public gathering, other than churchgoing. Even the children were no longer allowed to go guising at Halloween. The fact that people went along with these strictures shows how pervasive the idea of being the Chosen People was. Besides, ministers and church officers were encouraged to spy on parishioners to ensure that they were sticking to the rules. It is easy to see where the stereotype of the dour, humourless Scotsman started. If we had to live under a regime like that, we would probably all turn out like Private Fraser from *Dad's Army*!

You very rarely, if ever, read of anyone from the upper or professional classes being chained up or forced to wear the horrible scold's bridle. Most likely those with money were able to pay a fine rather than have to go through the pain and humiliation that the poor had to. It is doubtful too that anybody dared to check to make sure the rich were not drinking and dancing. The continuing importation of claret from France after the Reformation[3] suggests that the rich did not give up their drinking habits; nor were they forced to.

And yet, the Church of Scotland has long boasted of its democratic structures. Bishops were replaced with presbyteries, composed of elders, who were ordinary members of the surrounding church communities. Each church, moreover, chose its own minister, instead of one being appointed from on high. Ministers and elders were chosen by the local community to attend an annual General Assembly, which was the government of the Church.

The Church of Scotland supposedly worked as a democracy while the state was being run by elites. In the workings of the Church is seen the beginnings of the Scottish love of democracy and the Church is viewed as seminal in the development of the Labour Party and the Co-Operative movement.

Although in theory the Church of Scotland *was* a democratic institution, in practice, this was far from true. In rural parishes it became the norm for the local laird to choose the minister, rather than the congregation. In fact, this system was made law both by the Scottish Parliament and, after the Union of 1707, by Westminster.[4] Even in urban parishes town and burgh councils had the right to appoint ministers. So much for democracy!

And what about the presbyteries? Again, in theory, these were democratic, composed as they were of elders from the local area. It is hard to imagine that ordinary, working-class men, and they were all men, would have any chance of being made an elder. Elders were pillars of the community and it would have demeaned the office for there to be elders dressed in rags and walking about in bare feet.

Elders were chosen from men that were *already* pillars of the community; doctors, lawyers, businessmen etc. This, of course, made perfect sense since Calvinist doctrine said that the successful and well-to-do were fuller of God's Grace than others. Such men *should* be running the Church.

The wealthy showed their dominance of the Church in other ways too. They paid for private pews, which were sometimes boxed off, so that they did not have to mingle with the common herd. They also participated in something that no Protestant, and certainly no Calvinist, should ever have done.

Since Calvinist doctrine was clear that Purgatory did not exist, there was no need to get people to pray for you when you died. In fact, since you were one of the Elect, your place in Heaven was already guaranteed. Gravestones, therefore, were no longer necessary. Calvin and Knox certainly practised what they preached in this respect; nobody knows where Calvin is buried, while Knox's grave lies beneath a car park in Edinburgh. Wealthy Scots, however, refused to follow their example.

Thousands of tourists flock to Greyfriars Kirk in Edinburgh every year to see where Greyfriars Bobby is supposed to have mourned his master. Of more genuine historical interest are the iron bars on some of the graves, put there to stop grave robbers. As the tourists walk around the churchyard, they cannot fail to be impressed by some of the elaborate tombs on display. Nobody, though, stops to think of the fact that the tombs and headstones should not be there.

Ostensibly, the Church of Scotland did not want its churchyards cluttered up with unnecessary gravestones, but a way was found to let the wealthy have their way. The Church levied a fine on burials and memorials in churchyards. Presumably, the bigger the memorial, the bigger the fine would be. In practice, this meant that the well-to-do simply handed over cash to erect memorials to the deceased. It is not clear why they wanted these headstones and tombs; maybe they were hedging their bets in case the Church was wrong and Purgatory really did exist!

Poor people tend not to leave behind historical records, so it is hard to gauge how ordinary churchgoers felt about this dominance of the wealthy in their place of worship. Presumably they took comfort from the knowledge that, no matter how poor or insignificant they were, they were still part of the Elect and were among God's Chosen People.

Strangely, it was the penance inflicted upon the poor that verified their place among the Chosen People. This penance was not like that dished out by Catholic priests in the old days; remember, Protestant soteriology said that there was nothing that human beings could do to contribute to their own salvation. So, if the Church was not offering absolution for sins, then what was the point of doing penance?

The wearing of the 'jougs' and the scold's bridle, having to stand outside the kirk in sackcloth in full view of the people entering and sitting on the 'Repentance Stool' were public demonstrations of your sins against the *community*, not God. Your salvation was already secure as one of the Elect, but transgressions against God's community had to elicit a show of repentance. Eventually, you were welcomed back since, of course, you were one of the Chosen.

Being a member of the community was held to be so important that the ultimate sanction for recidivists was banishment.[5] This was a lot worse than it sounds since one's position as one of the Elect depended upon being a member of God's community. Banishment cast doubt on the very fact of one's elected status. The only way of feeling like one of the Elect again was to find another community to join; no easy task since, in most places, strangers were few and far between.

One of the other great myths of Reformation Scotland is that the establishment of schools for all (mainly boys) led to a more educated population.[6] This has been proven to be nonsense by various historians.[7] TC Smout is especially scathing about Scottish education. Essentially, education, as it always had been, was for the sons of the wealthy, especially at secondary and tertiary level. Ordinary children were given nothing more than a basic education; a very basic education.

People of my generation, who went to an RC school, might remember the catechism we were taught, and tested on, in the 1960s.

> Q: Who made me?
> A: God made me.
> Q: Why did God make me?
> A: God made me to know Him, to love Him and to serve Him in this world so that I may be happy with Him forever in the next.

I learned that when I was seven or eight and it has stuck with me ever since. There was a whole book of these questions and answers, but those first two were all I learned. For some reason, the whole thing was abandoned and never heard of again.

Back in the day, all the main churches had catechisms. They were apparently invented by Lutherans and, when they seemed to work, the idea was copied by the Catholic Church and other Protestant churches, including the Church of Scotland. It was basically Doctrine for Dunces, learned by rote by people that would not be able to understand real church teaching. This, of course, meant the poor.

In Church of Scotland schools, the catechism,[8] would be literally beaten into poorer children; God forbid they should be taught to read the Bible and debate about it. They might learn some rudimentary reading but nothing that would raise them above their current station. Still, so long as they learned that they were part of God's Chosen People, then it was job done.

One sometimes wonders if there have been attempts at a bit of social engineering in Scotland. It sounds like tinfoil-helmet stuff, but the Church of Scotland has always been quite a sophisticated organisation; it invented a method of torture, known as sleep deprivation, which is still used by repressive regimes and organisations today. It certainly would not have been beyond its capabilities to make sure the working classes were compliant and easily led.

For those that deny that there is any such thing as social engineering in schools, I encountered it myself and you probably have too without realising. I remember, in the 1960s, how we were constantly told to roll our 'r's. Most of the children in the class, including myself, found this quite difficult, but the teachers were adamant and, after being threatened and cajoled, we finally managed it. I went to a Catholic school, but it was also a state school and I would imagine that the Non-Denominational school down the road imparted the same instructions to *their* pupils.

Throughout primary school and into secondary, I often wondered what the point of this was; none as far as I could see. And then I went to university. Not one of the middle-class students I encountered, most of whom had gone to fee-paying schools, rolled their 'r's the way I had been told. In fact, quite a few of them could not pwonounce the letta pwoppelly at all. Everybody that was from a working-class background prrrrronounced their 'r's in exactly the same way I did. I find it hard to believe that this was simply coincidental.

So, the Church of Scotland was producing generations of knuckle-draggers, who were convinced that wealthy people were better than they were and favoured by God. Of course, these ignorant bruisers were also taught that they themselves were better than those outside of their church. It was as if the Church was looking to the future and breeding a class of cannon-fodder, ready to fight for the faith.

It is quite difficult to convince folk of their superiority if there is nobody they can point to as being inferior. The obvious candidate was the Catholic. There were still Catholics in Scotland after the Reformation, but they were left well alone and learned to keep their heads down. This suited the Church of Scotland since it could persuade its cohorts of knuckle-draggers that all 'indigenous' Scots were Protestants. Any Catholic threat would come from abroad.

There is a magazine in America called the *National Enquirer*, which specialises in feeding nonsense to the gullible. I first heard of it in the 1980s and assumed that it would be like the *Sunday Sport*, which went out of its way to peddle stories that were obviously fake. Front-page 'news' like a double-decker bus being found at the North Pole, a WWII plane being discovered on the moon and Hitler still breathing and living as a woman were evidently not intended to be taken seriously. The *National Enquirer*, however, was a different beast entirely.

The copy I read had a story about how teenagers in Britain were following a new craze: dressing up as characters from the *Rocky Horror Show*. There were plenty of quotes and pictures to back up what the magazine, quite seriously, was telling its readers. Surely, though, people would not be stupid enough to fall for this stuff? But one has to remember that the target audience for this magazine was one that would never be able to afford to go to Britain and find out for itself.

Similarly, the poorer among the Church of Scotland's congregation could be told anything about Europe's Catholics and they would believe it. If they had been told that the Catholics of France, Spain and Italy were creatures with four arms and six legs and breathed fire, they were hardly in a position to prove otherwise. As it was, they were subjected to terrifying stories of Jesuits being trained to come to Scotland and murder them all in their beds. They would then either eat the murdered Scots' children or, worse, take them off to Rome to be turned into Catholics.

This notion of the 'threat from abroad' is perfectly illustrated in the story of John Ogilvie. Although originally from Scotland, Ogilvie was educated in Europe and joined the Jesuits in France. When he returned to bring Scotland back to the fold, he easily fitted the stereotype of the foreign Catholic devil. Ogilvie was tortured and publicly executed, but his Scottish followers suffered nothing worse than a few nights in jail and a fine.[9] Everybody could then go back to pretending that Catholicism did not exist in Scotland.

As one might expect, this seething mass of uneducated, paranoid but supremacist humanity was going to need some kind of outlet. Any resentment they had against the wealthy was offset by being taught that these characters had been chosen by God to be their betters. They had also been taught to hate, but their hate-figures were mere phantoms; bogeymen that were making their evil plans abroad. They were going to need something more concrete to hate. During the Seventeenth Century, and the following centuries, that concrete hate-figure was provided.

We can look back in history, imagine the dour faces of the Scottish Presbyterians and compare them with those of the English: celebrating Christmas, dancing round maypoles; just dancing. It is rather easy to portray the Scots as being far more bigoted than the English and that is what many have done. The truth, however, is the complete opposite.

The reason why the English were more bigoted than the Scottish is quite easy to discern. The story of Jenny Geddes, whether apocryphal or not, gives a massive clue. Her cry of 'daur ye say Mass in my lug?'[10] was not, as is often claimed, because there was an actual *Mass* being said; it was an Anglican service. To Protestants outside of England, however, it was difficult to see the difference.

Although the Church of England was nominally Protestant, England had not really had what could be called a Reformation. Henry VIII might have broken with the Roman Church, but he was still a Catholic at heart and he executed plenty of Protestants to prove it. The Church of England ended up a mish-mash of different inputs under Henry, Edward VI and Elizabeth I. There was still a whiff of the Roman Catholic about the Church of England; something that created a problem both for its congregation and those in charge.

The only way that England could show that it was a true, Protestant nation was, unfortunately, to be more bigoted than anyone else. The English also had something that the Scottish lacked: real Catholics to express their hatred toward. These Catholics did not live in England, however; they lived in Ireland. The English had been trying to subdue the Irish for centuries and now the Scottish were going to be dragged into this mess.

James VI of Scotland was brought up with regular beatings and folk roaring in his ears about his duties and responsibilities as a Protestant monarch. As soon as he was old enough, he fought back and tried to make the Church of Scotland what he wanted it to be. With all the trouble this caused, along with his lack of cash, he could not wait to get down to London as soon as Elizabeth I died. He stayed in England the rest of his life, only making one, brief visit to Scotland.

James had his problems in England as well, but it was his third kingdom, one he had inherited along with England, that caused the most trouble. That kingdom was Ireland and James and his advisors decided to do something about it. Their solution was simply to throw Protestants at the problem. This was the famous, or infamous, *Plantation of Ulster*.

Those that moved from Scotland to Ulster had already been primed for bigotry and now, here they were, surrounded by real, live Catholics, all of whom were angry about their land being stolen from them. The paranoia they had been imbued with now had a focus. But those Scots living in Ulster were not the only ones to get dragged into Ireland's troubles. The whole nation ended up involved as well.

Charles I seemed to make it his business to rile everybody up. He tried to foist Anglicanism onto the Church of Scotland, annoyed English Puritans with his 'Divine Right' attitudes and angered Parliament with his autocratic rule. His actions led to the *Wars of the Three Kingdoms*, much of which took place in Ireland.

While Cromwell ruled, the English got a taste of what life was like in Scotland and they did not like it one bit. No dancing, no drinking, no feasting, no singing, no Christmas; no fun at all. No wonder there was mass rejoicing when Charles II took the throne. Unfortunately, the Restoration meant more trouble for the Scottish Presbyterians.

Charles II decided to resume his father's policies in Scotland and, when many Presbyterians defied his orders and stuck by the Covenant of 1638,[11] he sent in the troops. The majority of Scottish Presbyterians supported the Covenanters, even if they were too scared to attend their open-air services. Charles's Government in Scotland then raised a large army of Highlanders, many of whom were probably Catholics, to hunt down Covenanters in the southwest of the country.[12] These Highlanders were billeted on known Covenant sympathisers and were given licence to pillage and murder. This period became known as the *Killing Time*. For the first time ever, Scottish Protestants were faced with a Catholic threat from their own countrymen.

Matters were made worse in 1685, when Charles died, and his brother James became King. James had converted to Roman Catholicism, which made his decision to continue his brother's policies in Scotland appear extremely suspect. The *Highland Host* was long gone before James came to the throne, but they had left behind bitter memories. Besides, there were still troops hunting down and killing Covenanters. Now, however, they were doing it in the name of a Catholic king.

In 1687, James enacted the Declaration of Indulgence, which removed legal barriers that encumbered those that were not members of the Church of England.[13] This apparent attempt at religious freedom and tolerance hardly squared with the fact of all those Presbyterians being slaughtered in Scotland. As if that were not bad enough, he decided to extend religious freedom to Catholics in Scotland; which was not going to endear him to Scottish Protestants.

In England, the worry was that he was trying to force the country back to Catholicism. His extension of religious and civic freedom to Nonconformists was bad enough; the memory of life under Cromwell was still raw. The same right to religious and civic freedom to Catholics, however, was a move too far. He had also promoted Catholics to various positions of power. The last straw came when his wife gave birth to a baby boy. A Catholic dynasty was the last thing anyone wanted; it was time for James to go.

You would have thought that everybody had had enough of the Stuarts by this point, but they invited James's daughter to take over the throne. Mary was an Anglican and was married to the Dutch prince William of Orange, who also happened to be James's nephew. It shows how much loyalty there is in royal families that William and Mary did not have to be asked twice. You would never have seen a Habsburg stab a family member in the back like that! They invaded England with a small force and James fled to France. Scotland was happy to accept the pair as its monarchs as well.

It is worth mentioning at this point that William would have been perfectly happy to keep the laws that his uncle had passed. He was no bigot and was currently involved in a war against France, with his allies including the Habsburg Holy Roman Emperor and the Pope. It was his involvement in this war, however, that stymied his efforts at tolerance. The English Government refused to hand over any cash unless William agreed to the Bill of Rights,[14] parts of which limited the power of the monarchy. Of course, the Government refused to extend religious rights as far as William would have liked; and especially not to Catholics.

James decided that he was going to fight to get his throne back. He was backed by the French king, Louis XIV, who was keen to have another go at William and his allies. As was becoming customary, the war would take place in Ireland, allowing the English, forever after, to call William's coup a 'Bloodless Revolution.' Irish blood, whether Catholic or Protestant, obviously did not, and does not, count.

The depiction of this war in Ireland that we have all come to recognise is one of William, astride a magnificent white steed, single-handedly chasing Catholics across the River Boyne. In reality, William would have been well back, overseeing the attack and would hardly, as an experienced and accomplished general, have made himself an easy target by dressing in finery astride a gleaming, white horse. He would certainly have been surrounded by the banners of his allies, the Habsburgs and the Pope. In fact, the Pope celebrated William's victory with a Mass![15]

Quite apart from the irony of the Pope being on the side of William of Orange, there was the matter of the position of the Scottish Presbyterians in Ulster. They might have been handed the best land in the province but, in many respects, they were treated not much better than Catholics were. Even when Scotland and England united in 1707, nothing really changed in Ulster. Scotland kept its own laws and Presbyterian Church, but Ulster was ruled directly from England, albeit through a parliament in Dublin.

Daniel Defoe, at the start of the Eighteenth Century, bemoaned how the Ulster Presbyterians

> should now be requited with so injurious a treatment as to be linked with the very Papists they fought

against...There will certainly be no encouragement to the Dissenters to join with their brethren the next time the Papists shall please to take arms and attempt their throats. Not but they may be fools enough as they always were to stand in the gap.[16]

Events in the Sixteenth and Seventeenth Centuries showed two things about the great mass of Presbyterians in Scotland and Ulster. Firstly, the idea that those in authority were their betters and must be obeyed had become deeply entrenched. Even when they were subjected to persecution, as they were in Ulster, they were still ready to rally to the 'cause'; even if that cause was not particularly beneficial to them.

At the same time, however, the poorer classes of Presbyterians in Scotland had proven that they were prepared to defy those in authority. In the space of a century, they had overthrown, or been complicit in the overthrowing of, three monarchs. Obviously, the authority they were prepared to obey was a matter of choice.

This choice, however, was not their own. We are not talking about professional people here, either in Scotland or in Ulster, but the knuckle-dragging dregs, who were brought up in the Church of Scotland, Chosen People mindset. The authority they had learned to obey had to come from within their own church. If the minister said fight, they fought; if the minister said obey those magistrates, they tugged their forelocks and obeyed. Conversely, if the Scottish Presbyterian elites decided that somebody was an enemy, ministers would be duty-bound to tell their congregations *not* to obey and they would duly comply.

It was a rather worrying trend that had been established, where the great mass of Presbyterians was ready to obey anybody that came from the right background and made the right noises. Meanwhile, the Highlanders had faded back among their damp, miserable mountains and Scottish Presbyterianism could continue unmolested. The only worry was what those evil Catholics might do to their Presbyterian brothers over in Ireland.

3
Let's Work Together

If the Highlanders had faded into the background, there was always the worry that they might venture south again. Now that Scotland and England were united under one parliament, the Highlanders were a concern to the English as well. In 1745, kilts appeared on the horizon yet again and the Lowlanders were terrified.

There is no point in going over the story of the Jacobite Rebellion; it is not relevant. What is relevant, though, is the aftermath. Bonnie Prince Charlie made his escape after the defeat at Culloden; the Highlanders he left behind were not so lucky. Highland dress, the Gaelic language, even bagpipes, were all outlawed. Meanwhile, roads were built, forts were constructed, and troops were billeted to made sure the Highlanders complied with the new laws.[1]

As a kind of sop to the Highlanders, Highland regiments were set up, in which Highland dress was allowed. These regiments were sent all over the British Empire, fighting in kilts to the sound of the bagpipes, both of which were banned for their fellow countrymen at home.[2]

Throughout the Eighteenth Century, the Highlanders were constantly persecuted and then came the Clearances.[3] The mass evictions left Highlanders landless and homeless. Many had no other option but to go to America as indentured servants; virtual slaves. The legacy of those times can still be seen in the vast, empty spaces in the North of Scotland. A whole culture had been wiped out.

Meanwhile, as already mentioned, the Presbyterians in Ulster were in an unenviable position. Yes, they were part of the Elect, yes, they had real, live Catholics to look down on, but they were treated as second-class citizens by the Anglican members of the Church of Ireland. They had to pay tithes to this Established Church and had no say in how the province was governed. In many ways the situation was like it had been in Scotland before William and Mary arrived.

As the Eighteenth Century wore on, things got worse for the Ulster Presbyterians. By the second half of the century most intelligent people, especially in England, considered religious bigotry to be *so* Medieval. Moves were made to allow freedom of worship and economic rights; both of which affected Ireland as well. This was the last thing the Ulster Presbyterians wanted.

Not all Catholics were dirt-poor, and Presbyterians found themselves having to compete for leases on land with Catholics that might well outbid them. And the Catholics that *were* poor were now able to go after jobs that had previously been the sole preserve of Protestants. Of course, destitute Catholics were willing to work for less than Protestants were; even a pittance was more than they were used to having.

As you might expect, this caused tension all over Ulster and, in the 1790s, this erupted into violence. Gangs of Protestants attacked Catholics and gangs of Catholics attacked Protestants. One wonders, though, how much Anglicans were involved in all this. Rather unhelpfully, any narrative about these times always insists on using the word *Protestant*. Presumably, though, there were plenty of lower-class Anglicans around, who would be just as annoyed as the Presbyterians about Catholics having rights.

It is probable as well that the Catholic gangs did not distinguish between Anglicans, Presbyterians or anybody else. To them, they were all as bad as each other and had helped to keep down Catholics in Ulster for nearly two centuries. So, perforce, Anglicans were now viewing Presbyterians, not as inferiors, but as fellow Protestants, battling against the Catholics.

A rather curious aspect of this gang warfare between Catholics and Protestants was that the gangs organised themselves into societies, modelled on Freemasonry. This helped to legitimise the gangs, at least in their own eyes, and made it seem that they were actually fighting for some kind of cause. It seems that existing Masonic societies got involved in all this as well.[4]

Out of the Protestant side of these developments came a new organisation, named after William III; the Orange Order. Although this group, like all the others, modelled itself on Freemasonry, it was detached from the Masons; this was to be a decidedly lower-class organisation, free from interference from the upper and middle classes.[5]

The Orange Order, at least in its early days, sounds in some ways more radical and revolutionary than the United Irishmen. Being revolutionary and bigoted might seem mutually exclusive, but that is not the case. Bear in mind that the French Revolution was in full swing at this time, and it was from France that most radicals took their ideas.

It is a fact that is often overlooked in accounts of the French Revolution: its anti-clericalism. To the leaders of the French Revolution, the Catholic Church was just as oppressive as the nobility and attempts were made to remove it. Churches were closed, and priests were exiled and killed.[6] To an uneducated and illiterate, or semi-literate underclass, looking on from abroad, it might seem that anti-Catholicism was the whole point of the Revolution.

In the midst of this sectarian feuding, at the end of the 1790s, the United Irishmen attempted an ill-fated uprising, which was supposed to have been backed by Revolutionary French forces. As they always did, the Westminster Government sent in the troops. Atrocities were committed by both sides and, eventually, fearing more trouble, the Dublin Parliament was persuaded to vote itself out of existence and Ireland came under the direct rule of London.

Much is made about the fact that the United Irishmen was composed of Catholics and Protestants; Anglicans, Presbyterians and other Nonconformists of all shades. It would be a lifetime's work trying to piece together the denominations of everyone involved in the United Irishmen and, even then, in many cases it would prove to be a hopeless task. We can, however, make postulations from what we know about some of the leaders.

Theobald Wolfe Tone was an Anglican,[7] but others are merely described as 'Protestant'. It is possible to deduce, however, that Cornelius Grogan was most likely an Anglican as well, since his father was a member of the Irish Parliament.[8] Bagenal Harvey's father was one of the Court of Chancery's Six Clerks,[9] which would suggest that Harvey was an Anglican too.[10] But surely there must have been some Presbyterians involved?

Actually, it seems that it was Presbyterians that started the Society of United Irishmen in the first place.[11] Of course, Presbyterians do not just come from Scotland, so what we want to determine is the involvement of *Scottish* Presbyterians. The obvious answer to any question about Scottish Presbyterian input into the United Irishmen is that William Drennan was one of the founders of the organisation.

As a graduate of Glasgow University, which university his father, a Presbyterian minister, also attended, it was clear that Drennan had strong links with Scotland. The First Presbyterian Church of which Drennan's father was minister, however, was distinctly *not* of the Scottish variety. It had its own, liberal agenda and a radical outlook, which it still has to this day.[12] William Drennan, unfortunately, has led us down a dead-end.

Much more informative, for our purposes, is the fact that most of the Presbyterian members of the United Irishmen were middle-class, especially in Ulster.[13] (William Drennan, incidentally, was a physician.) Throughout Ireland, however, according to Tone's own, albeit rough, figures, Catholics in the United Irishmen outnumbered Protestants of every denomination by more than two-to-one.[14] Essentially, middle-class Protestants were the leaders of the United Irishmen, while lower-class Catholics provided the soldiers.[15]

Not surprisingly, most of the Catholic gangs participated in battles against British troops, alongside the United Irishmen. One gets the impression, however, that these Catholics were being used by the United Irishmen. Wolf Tone said of the Irish Catholics that they had been 'trained from their infancy in a hereditary hatred and abhorrence of the English name, which conveys to them no ideas but those of blood, pillage and persecution'.[16] That hardly makes it sound as if Tone was on the side of Irish Catholics.

In fact, among the leaders of the United Irishmen anti-Catholicism was prevalent. They saw the Catholic Church as counter-revolutionary, just like their counterparts in France.[17] William Drennan, for example, said that Catholics were 'unfit for liberty'.[18] This attitude was not helped by the Catholic Church in Ireland condemning the United Irishmen's rebellion.[19]

The other side of the coin, of course, was that France was a Catholic country, so the Revolution could be viewed as a *Catholic* one. This certainly appeared to be the attitude of members of the Catholic *Defenders* gangs.[20] And if Catholics thought that, you can be sure that Protestants did too and were prepared to fight accordingly.

The Orange Order, then, would have been a mixture of those thinking they were fighting against Catholic revolutionaries and those believing they were fighting against Catholic *counter-*revolutionaries. Of course, there would also have been those that did not give a damn about revolutions; they either just hated Catholics or wanted to maintain Protestant supremacy.

As we have already discussed, lower-class Presbyterians in Scotland were taught that they had to follow their betters and the Ulster Presbyterians, originally coming from Scotland as they did, were no different. They were incapable of thinking or acting for themselves. The Orange Order was bound to fall into the hands of its social superiors, sooner rather than later.

It only took about a year or so for the Orange Order to be taken over by the gentry and the Orangemen were put into battle against the United Irishmen by the British Army [21] The Orange Order was imbued with the spirit of the Protestant Ascendancy and the fight against the United Irishmen reflected that, as one of the songs from the period illustrates:

> Oh, croppies ye'd better be quiet and still
> Ye shan't have your liberty, do what ye will
> As long as salt water is formed in the deep
> A foot on the necks of the croppy we'll keep[22]

Since Catholics made up most of the visible face of the United Irishmen, the British were able to spread propaganda saying that it was simply a Catholic organisation, out to murder Protestants. So, while the United Irishmen were using Catholics, the British were similarly using Protestants.

Historian Jim Smyth says that 'All Protestants, whatever their doctrinal opinions were welcome to join the (Orange) order, although in practice Episcopalians outnumbered Presbyterians.'[23] From that it can be gauged that the lines between Presbyterians and Episcopalians, at least in Ulster, were becoming blurred. Now, they no longer looked at their differences, but at their common enemy. They were all *Protestants* now.

According to the Orange Order's own History, Scottish soldiers joined the Order and set up their own lodges when they came home.[24] They would also have brought back the message that Ulster was no longer divided between Anglicans and Presbyterians; it was now a case of *Protestants*, standing together against the murderous, Irish-Catholic hordes.

Ever since the Reformation took place in Scotland, one's Scottishness was defined by being a member of the Church of Scotland. When the Stuart monarchs tried to enforce an Episcopalian system in Scotland, it was Presbyterianism, rather than the Church itself, that characterised what it meant to be Scottish. The Covenanters saw themselves as distinctively Presbyterian and distinctively Scottish. That was changing now.

Protestants in Ulster, along with their fellows in Scotland, might be angry about having to have economic parity with Catholics and about seeing said Catholics openly celebrate their faith, but there was another matter about which they were even more incensed. It went to the very heart of living in what they believed to be a Protestant country.

As mentioned earlier, attitudes were changing in the Eighteenth Century, which meant that those in government were more willing to try different solutions to their problems. In the early 1790s, British fear of insurrection in Ireland, inspired by the French Revolution, made them think outside the box for a change. Instead of just getting stuck in with the muskets and cutlasses, William Pitt's government persuaded the Dublin Parliament to give the vote to Irish Catholics. This duly happened in 1793.[25]

Britain in the Eighteenth Century was nothing like a democracy and neither was Ireland; the 1793 measure did not change things much. Property qualifications made sure that only well-to-do Catholics got the vote. That, however, was no consolation to Ireland's Protestants. As far as they were concerned, no Catholic should be able to vote; and certainly not when there were so many disenfranchised Protestants.

This must have hit the Ulster Presbyterians especially hard. Here they were, God's Chosen People, not allowed to even choose their own M.P.s, while godless, superstitious Papists could now boast of having that right. No wonder they were so keen to riot, fight and join bigoted societies.

As Scottish soldiers came home and brought the Orange Order with them, so the outrage at the 1793 Act increased. It was not just a shared anger with their fellows in Ulster; the fact was that there were middle-class Protestants in Scotland and, indeed, in the whole of Great Britain, who did not have the vote while Catholics in Ireland of the same social class did. There was more than a whiff of unfairness about it all.

Even more frightening was the thought that the vote might be extended to Catholics in Great Britain. When Ireland was annexed to be ruled directly from Westminster, those fears were magnified. Pitt had promised further rights for Catholics in Ireland, including their being allowed to become M.P.s, to garner support for the Union with Britain. This, however, was stopped by the King, George III, who wanted no concessions to Catholics since he believed it violated his Coronation Oath.[26]

Pitt resigned soon after and the issue of further Catholic emancipation faded into the background. It was still talked about, though, often in public, and it remained as a possibility that haunted the dreams of many Protestants.

Sydney Smith, a renowned cleric, preacher, lecturer on moral philosophy and writer, wrote in his famous *Peter Plymley's Letters*,

> Nothing would give me such an idea of security, as to see twenty or thirty Catholic gentlemen in Parliament, looked upon by all the Catholics as the fair and proper organ of their party.[27]

From a member of the Protestant clergy, albeit an Anglican, to say such a thing was tantamount to treason for many. The man had even preached in an Episcopal church in Edinburgh for a few years and was a regular contributor to the *Edinburgh Review*. How could he let down his own people like that?

Actually, Smith's books were extremely popular and his articles in the *Edinburgh Review* were always eagerly anticipated. Indeed, many people bought the *Review* specifically to read Smith's articles.[28] Of course, not everyone would agree with his views; most enjoyed his wit and his effective use of irony. The point was, though, that his opinions on Catholic Emancipation were *tolerated*. To Orangemen, they should have been enough to have him sent to the Tower.

In the Orange Order's own History, it is said that the Order in Scotland came under the leadership of the Grand Lodge of England, whose headquarters ended up in London. At this point the Order was known as the *Loyal Orange Institution of Great Britain*. The Institution worked with Ultra-Tories[29] to try to stop Catholic emancipation.[30]

This political coalition with the Ultra-Tories explains the antipathy shown by the Orange Order to what became the 1832 Reform Act.[31] While working-class people throughout Britain campaigned for reform, believing that they were going to benefit as well, members of the Orange Order campaigned against it. Obviously, the upper classes among the Ultra-Tories were pulling the strings and the Scottish Presbyterian underclass was simply doing what it was told, as it always had done.

The campaign against the Reform Bill was against the Whigs, which had become the party of reform. The Ultra-Tories were against any changes whatsoever. Three years earlier, however, these Ultra-Tories were fighting against their own party and dragged the Orange Order with them.

Robert Peel was a serious individual; so serious that Disraeli described his smile as being 'like the silver plate on a coffin'.[32] There was no denying, however, that he was totally committed to all the ideals of Toryism, including being a staunch opponent of Catholic emancipation. So bitter was his opposition in this respect that it earned him the nickname 'Orange' Peel.[33]

It came as something of a shock, therefore, when Peel, in 1829, introduced a Catholic Emancipation Bill in the House of Commons. The Duke of Wellington was Prime Minister, but he was in the House of Lords, so it was left to 'Orange' Peel to push the bill through the Commons. With the support of Whigs in the Commons and the prior agreement of King George IV securing a safe passage through the Lords, the Act was quickly passed.[34]

Just as in 1793, it was fear of an uprising in Ireland that inspired the Act. Middle-class Catholics in Ireland could vote and even stand for Parliament, but they were not allowed to become M.P.s. Daniel O'Connell, who had huge backing among Irish Catholics of all classes, forced the issue by standing for election in County Clare and winning. To Wellington and Peel, it was either Catholic Emancipation or rebellion. They chose the former.

Orangemen throughout Britain tried to stop Catholic Emancipation being passed but, as they bemoan, 'to no avail'.[35] To their horror, middle-class Catholics throughout the United Kingdom could now vote and become M.P.s. The only consolation was that the property qualification was increased, so it was a more limited electorate than the one Ireland had after 1793. This meant some Irish Catholics losing the vote, which must have cheered the Orangemen up, if only a little.

At the turn of the century, the Industrial Revolution was in full swing. The war with France was also occurring at the time, but that did not stop the factories. If anything, it was a boom time, churning out arms and uniforms for the best part of twenty-five years. The factories needed coal and lots of it, as well as the raw materials they used in production. The problem was that the infrastructure, such as it was, could not keep up with the pace. Horse-drawn wagons took days to travel even relatively short distances. A better method was required.

Canals were a great idea, getting coal and raw materials to the factories in a fraction of the time. Building them, however, was not so easy. To keep the waterway in as straight a line as possible necessitated cutting through hills, while even preparing the canal beds required huge gangs of men armed with picks and shovels. It was hard, back-breaking and dangerous work. Not everyone was suited to it and not everyone wanted to do it.

As well as the work being hard, the men were expected to be there every morning, following the route of the canal. It was hardly the kind of job where one could commute to and from home. The navvies, as they were called, would live in makeshift camps, moving every few days as the canal progressed. It was a hard life and only hard men could manage it.

Gangs of men were hired by a foreman, who would be paid by the contractor for all the men he had taken on. It was not unknown for foremen to abscond with all the wages on pay day, so the navvies had to be constantly on their guard. The foreman might well have a few thugs on his side, so the navvies had to be able to handle themselves in a fight. As you can imagine, these were not the type of men anybody wanted living near them.

As is usually the case when large groups of men live together, drink played a large part in their lives. Gambling was also popular, leading to arguments and, quite often, full-scale battles. Gangs of prostitutes followed the men as well, which also led to fighting. Police services at the time were rudimentary, meaning that the navvies were a law unto themselves. They terrorised large parts of Britain and everyone was always glad to see them go. Sometimes locals would fight with them as they drank villages dry and stole food from farms. The navvies, however, usually came out on top.

Of course, there were complaints galore about these characters, but nobody was interested; least of all the Government. People might demand that troops be sent in to sort the navvies out, but contractors were keen to get finished on time, egged on by company shareholders, desperate for the canal to be open to traffic so they could watch the money roll in. It was something that everybody was just going to have to put up with until the canals were finished.

An added dimension to the menace posed by the navvies was the fact that many of them were Irish. These Irishmen would come over to work on a specific project and then go home until the next one. These lawless navvies spawned the stereotype of the drunken Irishman, quick to take offence and ready to fight anybody at any time. Of course, all the fear and hatred of the navvies was directed at the Irish, who were blamed for all the excesses of the camp dwellers.

The whole of Great Britain heaved a sigh of relief when the canals were completed, and the navvies vanished. Their happiness, however, was short-lived. Barely were the canals finished when railways began to be built. The navvies returned and this time they were more widespread; the railways were going everywhere.

To the Scottish Presbyterians the navvies must have come as a complete shock. Nobody could tell if they were Catholic, Protestant or what. If anything, they were like heathens that no religion could control. They drank when they wanted, even on the Sabbath, and woe betide anyone that tried to stop them!

The navvies, however, were only a temporary evil, and one that everyone could appreciate the necessity of when they were able to get a train to almost anywhere. The wave of incomers that arrived after the navvies had gone for good, though, was a different matter entirely. This lot came to live here permanently.

A myth has been fostered that the victims of the Great Famine were welcomed with open arms and looked after. This, however, could not be further from the truth. These people were not coming to 'sign on' and benefit from state handouts; such a thing did not exist in those days. The only available measure of poor relief was the workhouse; and parish supervisors were extremely reluctant to take anybody in. The workhouse system operated in exactly the same way in Ireland, so these incomers would have been well aware that there would be no state assistance in Scotland.

As for charity, the Irish would also be aware of *Souperism*, and would have held out no hope of any help from that quarter. Besides, people in the Highlands had suffered as well from the potato blight and, yet, Lowland charities sent them seed potatoes. Even back then they would have been well aware that the soil was now contaminated and there was every chance that no crop would come from these seed potatoes. It was a rather cynical, self-satisfied move, with no concern for the starving people involved. The Highlanders were starving and needed to eat there and then; not wait for a new crop. They were unfairly berated for eating the potatoes they had been given.[36]

Glasgow alone sent 50,000 Famine refugees back to Ireland,[37] proving how unwanted they really were. Given such an unwelcoming environment, why did Irish people keep coming? The answer is simple; they were not coming to beg, they were coming to look for work.

Employers then, as now, looked to maximise their profits by keeping wages low. This was best achieved with a large workforce, mired in poverty, competing for any jobs going. These industrialists were the only ones that *did* actually welcome the influx of Irish. Starving and desperate, they were willing to work for a pittance at jobs that very few wanted to do.

Rather than admire this self-sufficiency, which mirrored the mythical 'Protestant Work Ethic', Scottish Protestants despised these incomers. (You will notice that I do not use the word 'immigrants'. Ireland at that time was part of the UK, meaning that the Irish were UK citizens, free to come and go as they pleased.) This contempt was even greater than that expressed toward the navvies and it had at its heart religious bigotry.

If the navvies had displayed all the religious piety of a bunch of prehistoric savages, the new incomers most decidedly did not. To Scottish Protestants, their behaviour was even more shocking than those earlier itinerants. They attended Mass openly, for everyone to see! There was no law forbidding the celebration of Mass anymore, but still... They even celebrated Catholic feast days, like Christmas. It was absolutely shocking behaviour.

Meanwhile, the Church of Scotland was facing some crises of its own. The Union with England had robbed the Church of much of its power and influence since the Government was now hundreds of miles away in London. The Disruption of 1843 meant that about a third of its clergy and congregation left to form the Free Church of Scotland. But those were not the only problems; it was facing competition.

Just as in England and America, Scotland was host to great and successful Revivalist movements in the Eighteenth and Nineteenth Centuries. Unfortunately, these did not necessarily benefit the Church of Scotland. Having lost its political influence and rent in two by the Disruption, the Church was powerless to stop other denominations making inroads into Scotland. Baptists, Methodists, Congregationalists and many others burgeoned throughout the Nineteenth Century.

And not all the incomers from Ireland were Catholics. Presbyterians were among them, of course, but so, too, were Anglicans. The latter gravitated toward the Scottish Episcopal Church, generating something of a revival in that institution. Even by the middle of the Nineteenth Century, Scotland contained a plethora of different churches.

The idea of being among God's Chosen People started to undergo a fundamental change in the Nineteenth Century among the poorer classes. The mass migration to the cities from the countryside affected how the Church of Scotland was viewed by many of the poor. There had always been a suspicion that the Church was more concerned with the well-to-do. In fact, as we saw earlier, it was practically a doctrine of the Church that God's Elect did well in this life. Conversely, those at the bottom of the heap could not help but feel that God might not want them. The Church did not go out of its way to disabuse them of this notion.

With the Church no longer having the political power it used to have, irreligion was not the concern of the state anymore. Poor people could have a long lie on a Sunday without any fear of reprisals; the days of the 'jougs' were long gone.[38] In fact, it seems that many poor people only attended church to benefit from relief in the days when it was administered by the Church. Once the state took over the running of poor relief, there was no reason anymore for these people to attend church services.[39] They were not missed; the mostly middle-class congregations did not want them there.[40]

This new irreligion was a problem throughout industrial Britain and churchmen that ventured into the dark rookeries of the poor often thought of themselves as 'missionaries', as if they were going to preach to heathens in some foreign land. And just as middle-class people would balk at black folk sharing their place of worship, so they felt about the poor in their slums. In both cases, it was preferable to just donate money and let some soft-hearted soul go in among the savages.

In the second half of the century, the gulf between poor Protestants and the Church became, if anything, even more pronounced. Not only Irish Catholics worked in the living hell that was the St. Rollox Chemical Factory in Glasgow. Protestants worked there too, as well as in the Copper Works and Steel Works in the same city. There were also Protestants living in the filthy slums of the Gorbals and Garngad alongside Irish-Catholic families. Many of them probably got along with their Catholic neighbours, feeling that they were all in the same boat. Others, though, wanted to stay separate; they were members of God's Chosen People, after all.

This underclass of apostates no longer felt distinctly Presbyterian; their church had practically disowned them, after all. The Orange Order admitted anyone that was a Protestant, so Presbyterians now mixed with those of other churches in a common cause. The Sottish Presbyterian underclass began to see itself in a completely different light: as *British* and *Protestant*. It still thought of itself as being God's Chosen, but this was now extended to *all* Protestants. Needless to say, those Protestants that were not nominally Presbyterian were happy to go along with this.

The last quarter of the century saw an upsurge in membership of the Orange Order. There is debate over whether this was due to Irish Protestants moving to Scotland or if it was driven by events.[41] There were certainly plenty of events going on that would have even a moderate Protestant's head exploding.

In 1878 the Catholic hierarchy returned to Scotland. To anyone normal, this only affected Roman Catholics, but we are not talking about normal people here. To Orangemen, this was the thin end of the wedge; the Vatican would be running Scotland before too long. Quite why the Pope would be so desperate to take over Scotland nobody bothered to explain. Then there were Gladstone's Land Acts, which gave Irish-Catholic tenants the long-called-for 'Three Fs', fair rents, freedom of sale and fixity of tenure,[42] followed by his attempts to pass Irish Home Rule through Parliament. It was enough to give any self-respecting Orangeman apoplexy.

It might seem incongruous that a country that was so beset by sectarian bigotry was also the birthplace of the Labour Party. The Independent Labour Party grew out of various Scottish radical groups as well as the Trades Union movement. The electorate had grown considerably with the 1867 and 1885 Acts, which gave the vote to better-off working men, and many radicals and union leaders looked to give the working classes their own voice in Parliament.

As we saw in the United Irishmen Rebellion, radicalism and bigotry were not necessarily mutually exclusive. In the late Nineteenth Century this had not changed; all that was different was the excuse. Since Irish Catholics were poorly paid, it was easy to blame them for keeping the wages of manual labourers down. In a sense, this was true; but it was hardly the fault of the exploited Irish workforce. Nevertheless, it was clear that Socialism in Scotland was not for the benefit of everyone.

None of this, however, was of any great concern to the Protestant underclass, as we now must call them. None of them had the vote and very few, if any, were in a union; Trades Unions were exactly that – unions for men that had a trade. Just like the Irish Catholics, the men of the Protestant underclass were concerned with making ends meet and not much else; apart from hating Catholics, that is.

In some ways, the lack of a church was a liberating experience for the Scottish Protestant underclass. They were now free to indulge in the pastime that had been available to their peers in England since the Restoration of 1660: drinking. Alcohol was cheap and was one of the few pleasures that poor people could afford. Now that there were no ministers or elders to spy on them, the Scottish Protestant underclass could drink themselves silly.

There were various temperance societies active throughout Scotland in the Nineteenth Century, such as the Rechabites and the Band of Hope; testament to how much drunkenness there was. All of these tried to encourage working-class people to 'sign the pledge', give up the demon drink and become respectable. The International Order of Rechabites was run along the lines of Freemasonry,[43] which would obviously appeal to many Protestants. The Band of Hope reached out to younger people with marches, lectures, magic lantern displays and trips to the seaside.[44]

This drive for respectability also became part of the Orange Order. Although never officially espousing temperance, drunkenness was frowned upon and, apparently, you needed a letter of recommendation from a clergyman to join.[45] This would, effectively, rule out many of our Protestant underclass. There was nothing, however, to stop the underclass following Orange marches or standing on the sidelines cheering.

This is something that many observers, historians and sociologists, fail to take account of. They look at the fluctuating membership of the Orange Order, even during the Nineteenth Century, as evidence of the rise and fall of Orangeism. This fails to acknowledge, however, that there are many in Scotland that *support* Orange ideas, but do not necessarily wish to join the Order. This is a point we shall come back to.

Meanwhile, in 1872, an institution was born that would come to replace churches, and even the Orange Order, as the ultimate expression of one's Protestantism for the Scottish Protestant underclass.

4
People Get Ready

Football, in various forms, has a long history in Scotland, going back centuries. It was English, middle-class men, however, who gave us the game of Association Football. Its middle-class roots are still betrayed by the nickname used for it. 'I say, chaps, do you fancy a game of rugger? Or would you prefer a jolly old game of soccer?'

Football clubs sprang up all over England and, soon, Scotland as well. This growth was stimulated by working-class people, who had discovered that football was an excellent spectator sport. It was around this time, in the 1860s, that workers had won a half-day holiday on a Saturday. There was no better way to spend a Saturday afternoon than watching a football match. They were even willing to pay for the privilege.

For a couple of decades (longer in Scotland) the game had to be played by amateurs. There were, however, ways around this. Teams could attach themselves to local factories, where players would be offered a 'job'. Essentially, this was professionalism by the back door. Not that this concerned the spectators; they just paid their money and watched the match.

Scottish football was a snooty organisation, with the SFA resisting professionalism right up until 1893. Religious bigotry played its part as well. Hibernian FC used to get the blame for this as it had a Catholics-only policy from its inception in 1875. This, however, was due to the club being formed from the Catholic Young Men's Society.[1] In fact, religious bigotry in Scottish football predated the founding of Hibernian.

The real bigotry came in the shape of the founder of 3rd Edinburgh Rifle Volunteers (later called St. Bernard's) FC, one John Hope, a well-known anti-Catholic.[2] It seems that he was instrumental in the opposition to Hibernian being accepted into the Edinburgh FA, which subsequently stopped them being accepted by the SFA.[3]

Edinburgh, however, did not end up being the capital of bigotry in Scotland. That dubious honour fell to Glasgow. Of course, Glasgow and its surrounding area was where most of the Catholics from Ireland settled. It was also home to a sizable group of Ulster Protestants. The latter, however, were not solely responsible for all the bigotry; Scotland had plenty of bigots of its very own.

In 1872 a new Scottish team was founded in Glasgow. There was nothing remarkable about it; Hibs, Hearts and Partick Thistle were all founded in the 1870s. This team, called Rangers, was just another in the rapidly burgeoning Scottish game. After a rather itinerant existence, playing at different venues, Rangers finally moved to the Ibrox area in 1887.

The following year, John Ure Primrose was elected 'Patron' of Rangers, which some see as the beginnings of sectarianism at the club. Primrose was a well-known anti-Catholic, Conservative and Unionist, but that hardly means that the club was immediately guided in that direction. The story of Rangers officials being involved in the formation of Clydebank, a club that apparently 'expressed Unionist sympathies',[4] means nothing either. Supporting Unionism is hardly a crime and does not automatically mean that either club was a hotbed of sectarian bigotry.

There were plenty of people throughout the UK expressing Unionist sympathies at that period. Gladstone was advocating Irish Home Rule, which polarised politics totally. And Primrose at that time was a mere councillor,[5] not the man of influence he was to become later. He would not have been dictating how a club would be run; that was still to come.

In the same year that Primrose became the Patron of Rangers, 1888, another club started up in Glasgow. Founded by Brother Walfrid of the *Marist Brothers of the Schools*, a teaching order, the purpose of the club was to raise money to alleviate poverty among the Irish Catholics of Glasgow's East End. Such charity was badly needed.

There were plenty of charities in Glasgow catering for the poor and low-paid, run by churches and religious organisations. Religious bigotry probably played some part in the lack of provision for the Irish-Catholic poor, but there were other difficulties as well. Historians still argue about how widespread *Souperism* was during the Great Famine in Ireland, but nobody can argue that the *perception* of it caused a lot of mistrust.[6] Irish Catholics had learned not to trust Protestant charities, and this probably stopped many from accepting relief in their new home.

There was another problem caused by this perception, which came about due to the scandal that the practice caused in Britain. The newspapers made it seem as if *Souperism* was widespread and that *all* churches were involved. Such was the embarrassment caused by this that most churches were scared to offer relief to members of other *Protestant* churches, never mind Catholics.

The name of this new club was carefully chosen so as not to be overly Irish; the likes of *Hibernian* or *Harp* were deemed unsuitable. *Celtic* was chosen as a more neutral name, reflecting as it did both Irish and Scottish roots. Even the very choice of an association football club showed a willingness to integrate. The Gaelic Athletic Association could be pretty snooty about sports that were not indigenously Irish (it still is[7]), so Celtic were determinedly aligning themselves with *British* sports.[8]

It is clear that neither Celtic nor Rangers were founded along sectarian or bigoted lines; it obviously developed later. Billy Murray, in his book The Old Firm, argued that it was Celtic's success that resulted in hatred of the club and subsequent religious bigotry.[9] Others take this argument further, saying,

'After the formation of their great rivals, Glasgow Celtic, in 1888, Rangers found themselves lagging behind the new side as Celtic took the Scottish footballing world by storm'.[10]

That, however, is nonsense. By the end of the Nineteenth Century, Celtic had won four League titles. Rangers were one behind but won in seasons 1900-1901 and 1901-1902 to make their total five. In the, at that time, more prestigious Scottish Cup, Celtic and Rangers ended the century on three wins each. That could hardly be called 'Rangers lagging behind', or Celtic taking the 'Scottish footballing world by storm'.

By 1909, though, Celtic were setting records, with six Scottish Cups and nine League titles to their name. Even then, however, there was no great hatred or bigotry coming from Rangers supporters. In fact, in the 1909 Scottish Cup Final replay, both sets of supporters worked together in a riot at Hampden Park. When the replay ended in a draw, the supporters suspected that both clubs were working together to milk as much money as they could.[11] A riot might not seem the best example of 'working together' but at least they were not blaming or fighting each other!

And yet, in 1909 there was plenty for Scottish Protestants to be riled about. Three years earlier, the Liberal Party had won by a landslide, mainly due to popular anger at the policies of the

Conservative Party and their Liberal Unionist allies.[12] Most of Scotland had voted Liberal[13] but to Protestant Unionists this presented a huge problem; Irish Home Rule was sill a major part of Liberal policy and they were bound to introduce it sooner or later.

It had to be said, however, that no mention of Irish Home Rule was made during the Liberal campaign of 1906. Instead, it was a negative one, calculated to appeal to the baser instincts of the working-class bigot.[14] A huge deal was made of the importation of Chinese 'coolies' to South Africa, with the implication being that the Tories were ready to do the same in the UK. And then there was the 1902 Education Act, which brought Anglican and Catholic Church schools into the English state system. 'Ratepayers money for Sectarian Schools,' said the Liberals.[15] One can just imagine how Scottish Orangemen, and Protestants in general, felt about that!

The Scottish Protestant underclass, however, did not have a vote. The UK was not yet a democracy; only the better-off among the working classes had been granted the franchise, while women of all classes could not vote in Parliamentary elections at all. How this underclass felt about things is difficult, if not impossible, to gauge. No doubt they went along with whatever somebody in authority told them, as they normally did.

A major point about this period is that this seething mass of hatred and bigotry had no outlet. They could not vote, so political parties left them alone; Protestant churches did not want them stinking out their meeting-places and giving the more respectable among the congregation fleas, lice and God knows what else; and even the Orange Order, aiming for respectability to belie its bigotry, did not want these unthinking savages in its midst.

Of course, nobody could stop them following behind Orange parades, doing their funny walk and punching the sky, or standing on the pavement, cheering and singing, as the Walk passed. The Orange Order, however, always disowned this mob and blamed it for any trouble that occurred. This Protestant underclass desperately needed an organisation of its own. Unfortunately, they were too unintelligent and too used to following their 'betters' to organise anything of their own. Somebody was going to have to do it for them.

John Ure Primrose had come a long way from his days as a councillor. He had been a magistrate and a senior magistrate with

Glasgow Corporation and was Lord Provost between 1902-1905. He was also made a baronet when King Edward VII came to Glasgow in 1903.[16] And then, in 1912, he became chairman of Rangers Football Club. He still expressed anti-Catholic bigotry and 'publicly pledged Rangers to the Masonic cause'.[17]

This was a godsend to the Protestant underclass. Unwanted by churches and the Orange Order, they could now go to Ibrox, wear their scarves, sing their songs and feel that they were part of the hallowed order of Freemasonry. At last, they had a spiritual home, at a club whose chairman was determined to make it a hotbed of anti-Catholic bigotry.

Freemasonry in Scotland has long had a reputation for anti-Catholic bigotry; something its members have always tried to deny. It has invented a history for itself that goes away back to Medieval times but, strangely, they can only produce records that begin after the Reformation in Scotland. Still they persist with inventions about their origins, even sometimes claiming that they *had* records going back to the Middle Ages, which, unfortunately, got lost.[18]

They admit themselves, though, that many Masons are also members of the Orange Order,[19] which rather defeats their protestations of innocence somewhat. Even Masons that are not members of the Orange Order are well known for expressing anti-Catholic attitudes.[20] Most folk would agree that there is not much to choose between the two organisations.

For good measure, Primrose also instituted a sectarian signing policy at Rangers, excluding Roman Catholics from playing there. This policy outlived Primrose by more than sixty years, which showed how ingrained it became. The policy was never made official, but it escaped nobody's notice that Catholics were not welcome at Ibrox. It must have pleased the Scottish Protestant underclass no end.

As often happened in the Nineteenth Century with charitable institutions (Edinburgh's hospital schools are a prime example), Celtic ended up being run as a business. Since Celtic and Rangers came to dominate Scottish football by the end of the Victorian Age, they came to be known as the *Old Firm*. The perception was that the boards of both clubs would do anything, including collusion in fixing matches, to make money, which is what prompted the riot at Hampden in 1909. This idea of the *Old Firm* has been expanded by some people, who reach the conclusion that both Celtic and Rangers encouraged religious bigotry as a money-making scheme.[21] This, however, is nonsense.

If, indeed, there ever was a mutually beneficial agreement between Celtic and Rangers, it came to an abrupt end in 1912. The question that has to be asked is, would Primrose have instituted his bigoted policy at Rangers if Celtic had not existed? Considering the fact that he was an anti-Catholic bigot of long standing, voicing such views long before Celtic came on the scene, the answer has to be a resounding yes. That being the case, it is difficult to argue that Celtic had anything at all to do with the bigotry on display at Ibrox.

Andrew Sanders desperately tries to show that both Celtic *and* Rangers have been guilty of sectarian bigotry. His assertion, however, that Celtic played in the colours of Ireland, while the supporters sang Irish songs means nothing. Neither do the facts that Rangers' colours were red, white and blue and the supporters sang Unionist songs.[22] All that shows is partisanship. It was Rangers alone that brought hatred to the party; hatred of Catholics. It was a direct appeal to the lowest common denominator in Scottish society.

Now that the Scottish Protestant underclass had their very own church-cum-lodge, the next thing they needed was a name. There were those that had followed Rangers for years, long before Primrose appeared on the scene, and would still follow their team, simply as football supporters. What the Protestant underclass needed was something that would separate them from those that were merely Rangers supporters.

There is a phenomenon in schools in working-class areas that teachers refer to as the *Percolation Effect*. You only get to see this if you spend a long time, a couple of decades say, teaching at the one school. Gradually, the more intelligent, more skilful or more ambitious pupils move out of the area. This is a long, drawn-out process but, eventually, all that is left is the dregs; the unintelligent, those that are anti-education and who have few interests other than getting pissed, stoned or otherwise wasted. Trying to teach the offspring of these people can be nothing short of a nightmare.

If this phenomenon can be observed after just a few generations, imagine what it would be like after centuries. Actually, you do not need to imagine; Scotland has such a group, the result of over four-hundred years of filtration. We have traced their development from the Reformation to the Twentieth Century, by which time there was nothing left but the chaff.

Understanding the complexities of Protestant theology was well beyond the capabilities of this underclass. Even a catechism was too much. What they needed was a simple catchphrase; something that would sum up the whole Calvinist idea of the Elect. They were like the sheep in *Animal Farm*, who could not cope with the list of rules so were taught to parrot, 'Four legs good, two legs bad.' In the same vein, somebody taught the Scottish Protestant underclass to say, 'We are The People'. They took to this slogan eagerly, even though none of them really knew what it meant.

5
Church of the Poison Mind

Like any new religion, The People needed doctrines. There was no need to get the Bible out or hold intense, theological discussions, however; they already had everything they needed to hand. The catechism that had been thumped into them for generations provided all the doctrine they required. Okay, they did not quite understand all the ins-and-outs, but they had the basics.

Calvinist doctrine taught about the predestined salvation of the Elect, and how that Elect showed itself through belonging to the right church. The People adopted this and claimed that they were predestined to follow Rangers. Nobody could choose to have Rangers as his team; God had chosen His special football fans before time began.

> We do not choose, we are chosen. It's not just a leisurely way to spend a Saturday afternoon, an interest, no ...it's much much more than that, a calling, a duty, a lifestyle.
> Rangers are not an occasional intervention into our everyday lives, they invade our very core in an all-consuming way, from the cradle to the grave.
> Pause. Take a moment to take stock...and imagine how different our lives would have been had we not been one of the chosen.
> Doesn't really bear thinking about does it?[1]

It is worth reading the whole of this little diatribe online to get the full flavour of this belief. And this character is not alone; they all believe that God created Rangers for his Chosen People to gather together. There are no comments, however, regarding soteriology. For one thing, it is too big a word for The People to handle. Presumably, though, supporting Rangers guarantees one a place in Heaven.

An integral part of Calvinist doctrine, if you remember, one that set it apart from other Christian faiths, was that God shows favour to his Chosen People on earth as well as in Heaven. Members of the Elect are expected to do better than others in life; the more successful they are, the more favoured by God they obviously are.

The People transferred this doctrine to their team, which, it always had to be argued, was the most successful in Scotland, if not the world. To achieve this success was the be-all-and-end-all; the whole *raison d'être* of the team. Nothing else mattered; certainly not ethics.

When John Ure Primrose pledged Rangers to the Masonic cause, one has to ask why. Why the Freemasons? Why not Protestantism, or Unionism? A possible answer to that question is something that everyone associates with the Masons; doing each other favours. Did Primrose align Rangers with the Masons expecting certain folk to 'help the widow's son'?

There has always been a suspicion that match officials have been helping Rangers for many years; a flag for offside here, a missed foul there. In any penalty decision, Rangers always seemed to get the benefit of the doubt, whether through being awarded a penalty kick or the opposition not getting one that it deserved. It is always strenuously denied that this has been the case, but the fact that the idea of this occurring is so pervasive suggests that something untoward has been happening.

In more modern times, Rangers always, always appealed whenever a player was suspended. This occurred even when the player had obviously committed an infringement, even a violent one. This freed up the player to appear in an important match. On more than a few occasions, incidentally, those appeals were upheld, despite plenty of evidence to the contrary.

If Primrose was a huge influence on Rangers, another man practically moulded the club into what he wanted. That man was Bill Struth, who became manager in 1920. A control freak, who ruled autocratically for thirty-four years, Struth is often painted as being Rangers personified. The players' lives were ruled with an iron fist and they had to be clad in suits and bowler hats when they were not playing. Any player that broke Struth's rules would have his arse beaten with the business end of an oar, which had inadvertently broken off when Struth had been on a boating trip with a friend. (Well, maybe not, but the players certainly seemed to be frightened of him.)

With Struth's reputation the way it is, there are always efforts to argue that he had a 'soft side'.[2] This argument is difficult to sustain, however, when you consider that Struth's wife committed suicide in 1941. Apparently, she suffered from severe depression, but the excuse is always made that mental illnesses were not understood in those days.[3] That is nonsense. Great strides were made in the treatment of mental illness during the First World War and psychoanalysis had been around for a good while by the end of the 1930s. Probably the woman was hidden away to preserve Struth's image.

Struth's heartlessness was to the fore a decade earlier in the way he treated Sam English. My dad worked beside a couple of members of English's family in the shipyards in the 1950s and they said that the man was a nervous wreck for years after the incident with Johnny Thompson. It is certainly common knowledge that the player was severely traumatised, which caused his career to be cut short.[4]

For more than a decade before the accident with Johnny Thompson, doctors had been treating the victims of shell-shock, nowadays known as Post-Traumatic Stress Disorder. It would have been clear, even to the meanest quack, that English was suffering from the exact same illness. But English was not allowed any treatment, or even time off to come to terms with what had happened. Instead, Struth had him back on the pitch almost immediately. It did not matter if he was wandering around in a daze; as long as he could score the odd goal or fall down in the box for a penalty. Winning was all that mattered.

Struth's behaviour also had the effect of making Sam English appear to be a hard-hearted bastard. To be back playing so soon after Thompson had died made it look as if English simply did not care. Opposition supporters started shouting things like 'Murderer!' at him. Not that Struth cared. As long as it did not affect him or his precious club.

So, Struth only cared about his team winning and was not bothered who got hurt in the process. But, what about cheating? Would Struth condone breaking the rules in order to win? His attitude in this respect was made clear from a story he liked to tell about his days as a professional athlete. Apparently, at the time, he needed money and cheated in a race, so he could win the prize.[5] It is never mentioned exactly *how* he cheated, but somebody that showed such a flippant disregard for the rules would have no qualms about his team cheating in football matches.

Just as with Struth's story about the race, we have no idea how, or if, Rangers *did* cheat while he was manager. Those that could tell us are mostly dead, while it was something that the newspapers of the time would never report. All we have is tales about what a wonderful manager Struth was. His legacy became obvious in later years, however; cheating was not really cheating if it was Rangers that did it.

Struth's win-at-any-cost mentality even affected Rangers during WWII. This is a subject I covered before in my book *Damned Agnivores* and the evidence against the club is, indeed, damning.[6] Rangers apologists like to show the names of folk associated with the club that fought, and, in some cases died, in the War. There is no denying this, but nothing is ever mentioned about those that did *not* fight but stayed to make sure that Rangers dominated Scottish football.

Dougie Gray, Jimmy Smith, Alex Venters, Scot Symon and other pre-war stalwarts managed to still ply their trade at Rangers throughout the conflict. This was achieved by the simple expedient of Rangers players going to 'work' in the shipyards as soon as war was declared. Shipyard work was a reserved occupation, meaning that anyone in there would not be considered for conscription. Rangers apologists would attempt to point out that not everyone conscripted was sent off to war. This was true; ten percent of all those conscripted were sent down the mines. None of them, though, were sent to work in the shipyards.

A prime example of the Rangers policy was Willie Waddell, who 'was due to study dentistry but that was not a reserved profession so instead he ended up working in a shipyard'.[7] One needs to ask, by what possible process did he end up working in a shipyard? He was not a *Bevin Boy*; that would have meant working down a coalmine; besides, conscripts were not chosen for such jobs until 1943.[8] The only way he could have got a job in a shipyard was if somebody fixed it for him.

During the War, the normal leagues were abandoned, and temporary, regional leagues were set up. Most clubs could barely muster a team to put on the field for matches and relied on permitted 'guest' appearances by players that were posted to nearby army camps. Rangers, on the other hand, were able to field not one, but two teams in two separate leagues. Apparently, though, they had no unfair advantage.

In later years, there was a campaign for the titles won by Rangers during the War to be officially recognised.[9] Doing this might create a problem when it comes to the 1941-42 season. During that season, Rangers not only took part in two leagues, they won them both.[10] Instead of trying to count these 'titles', it should be a constant source of embarrassment that Rangers were able to do this, while others were off fighting the Nazis.

A bonus for Rangers was that once the war was over, they had a team that fitted this description of Willie Waddell:

> Rangers played in area divisional leagues during the war and Waddell was a regular and influential performer. They carried off all seven league titles played for in wartime and out of the 34 competitions they entered, they won 25.
> The result was that when the Scottish League resumed in 1946-47, Waddell was a highly experienced and gifted player.[11]

It was hardly a surprise, then, that Rangers were pretty dominant in the post-war years, right up until the first of Jock Stein's nine in a row.[12]

As can be deduced from the campaign to make the wartime titles official, Rangers and its supporters see nothing wrong with this shameful period. This was God's Chosen Team, supported by God's Chosen People, after all. They were predestined to do nothing but good, which translated to them being unable to do anything wrong, no matter what it was.

A symbiosis developed between The People and their club; while they were prepared to watch Rangers cheat everyone, the club returned the favour by ignoring, or even justifying, its supporters' lawlessness. The Masonic model was obvious.

And cheat the club most certainly did. In 1969, Willie Waddell became manager of Rangers. He had been Bill Struth's protégé, remember, as well as one of the 'Shipyard Shirkers'. He immediately, as Sandy Jardine related, instilled in the players 'what it means to be a Ranger' and made sure they 'understood the tradition and the heritage'.[13] If they did not understand what 'it meant to be a Ranger', they soon did.

John Greig, for example, told in his autobiography about Waddell approaching him before a match in the UEFA Cup Winners' Cup.

> The boss held up a photograph of one of the Torino players and said to me: 'John, this is their number one player, Claudio Sala. He is just 19 and he is the new Italian wonderboy. I want you to put him out of the game. I asked: 'Just for this one game, boss, or for good?' 'I'm serious, John,' he rapped and I replied: 'So am I, boss, so am I.[14]

One player that was not so keen on the Rangers style of play was David Smith, who, apparently, left 'Rangers for Arbroath in protest at (Jock) Wallace's instructions to boot his opponents.'[15]

And former Dynamo Moscow player Anatoly Baidachny remembers of *that* final in Barcelona: 'One of our players, Aleksandr Makhovikov, was absolutely taken out by a Rangers player on the wing. No whistle. From that, Rangers went up and scored.'[16]

And it was not only European teams that got roughed up by Rangers. John McMasters of Aberdeen had his head stamped on by Willie Johnston and needed the kiss of life.[17] And that was not the only time Johnston caused injury to another player. His excuse was quite pathetic:

> I would get my retaliation in first...People were kicking lumps out of us. It wasn't nice. They'd kick you to death. They were hurting you and making sure you were going to stay hurt. Off the ball, high tackles, attempts to break your leg.[18]

Strangely, those kinds of injurious tackles were the trademark of John Greig and were later emulated by Graeme Souness and Ian Ferguson. In later years, Alex Rae kicked into a player's head while he was lying on the ground.[19] This thuggery, however, was as nothing compared to the corporate fraud that Rangers perpetrated on Scottish football.

Unlimited funds from the Bank of Scotland, Discount Option Schemes, Employee Benefit Trusts; any ruse was employed just so Rangers could win. Of course, such chicanery could not last forever. The Bank of Scotland was taken over by people that subscribed to the rather strange financial belief that money loaned out should be paid back. Meanwhile, HMRC attempted to recoup all the tax that had been swindled. The jig was up.

As far as The People were concerned, however, their club had done nothing wrong. It was all a big conspiracy, cooked up by those nasty Catholics. As many of them have put it, Celtic could not beat Rangers on the pitch, so they tried to destroy the club altogether. The 'Unseen Fenian Hand' had infiltrated everything, including the banks, HMRC and other Government departments. The rot went right to the top; to the SFA and the SPL administrations; to the Scottish Government; even to the Westminster Government. The Vatican's tentacles were everywhere, and they were determined that Rangers would be destroyed.

Before those torturous days were reached, however, The People had already proven their unquestioning loyalty to the club that God had chosen for them. Even when the club acted in such a way that The People got hurt, they were ready always to forgive and forget; or blame somebody else.

The 1971 Ibrox Disaster was only the last in a culmination of incidents where people were seriously injured, and even lost their lives, at the stadium. In 1974, Sheriff Irvine Smith said,

> So far as the evidence is concerned, the Board never so much as considered that it ought to apply its mind to the question of safety on that particular stairway [...] and would appear – I put it no higher – to have proceeded on the view that if the problem was ignored long enough it would eventually go away [...] Indeed it goes further than this because certain of their actions can only be interpreted as a deliberate and apparently successful attempt to deceive others that they were doing something, when in fact they were doing nothing.[20]

Rather worryingly, Smith says, in a book about his life, that, even forty years after his judgment, 'he is viewed with disapproval by some Rangers-supporting friends, who accuse him of "disloyalty"'[21] One cannot help but wonder how he was treated by those Rangers supporters that were *not* his friends. The People have some pretty heavy-handed ways of dealing with those they consider enemies of their club. No doubt those that brought private cases against Rangers on behalf of their dead relatives suffered the same abuse.

Even though Rangers did not dispute Smith's findings,[22] The People have busied themselves ever since in looking to exonerate Rangers and shift the blame onto somebody else. The Hillsborough Disaster, eighteen years after that at Ibrox, has been pounced on as an example of football authorities not learning lessons from what had happened.[23] Even though a completely different set of circumstances led to the disaster at Hillsborough, The People would clutch at any straw to clear the name of their club, their church.

Rangers, of course, frequently had to return the favour as The People rampaged through every place their team played. So bad were the depredations inflicted by The People, not only in Scotland but throughout Europe, that they earned them the nickname they hate: *Huns*. Just like Attila and his hordes, The People spread terror wherever they went.

As early as the 1960s, Rangers supporters were already getting themselves a reputation for hooliganism. Even when it was a friendly, the Rangers fans seemed not to be able to help themselves.[24] In 1976, Rangers supporters ran rampage in Birmingham in what became known as 'Sick Saturday'. It is still the 'worst hooliganism Villa Park has ever seen'.[25]

The disgraceful scenes in Barcelona in 1972 only served to spread the vile reputation of The People further. Apparently, the hooliganism was not confined to the Nou Camp and there are stories of churches and shrines being vandalised by drunken mobs. This, of course, is denied by The People, but their behaviour in Birmingham four years later would suggest that there is some truth behind the stories.

Thirty-six years later, The People were still behaving in the same way. The team had reached the final of the UEFA Cup in Manchester and the supporters did their usual job of smashing up the city. In scenes of destruction that were described as 'one of the worst nights of violence since the Blitz',[26] shops and cars were vandalised, and policemen were attacked with bottles and other missiles. It was yet another shameful display by The People.

Incredibly, Rangers, and their friends in the media, have made excuses for the behaviour of The People no matter how extreme their acts. As you might expect, alcohol is blamed a lot of the time, while a lot of 'whatabootery' comes into it as well. For example, Willie Waddell, speaking about the trouble in Barcelona,

> argued that the police had over-reacted, that the fans were drunk but not intent on violence, and that recent European finals had witnessed rejoicing Celtic, Bayern Munich and Ajax fans running on to the park and those occasions had been deemed acceptable.[27]

Even at the time, attempts were made to shift the blame onto Franco's police.[28] This has since become the standard narrative. The problem with this argument is that the Catalan people of Barcelona were no friends of Franco; in fact, they hated him and his fascists. And yet, there are no instances of people from Barcelona blaming the police for what happened. Unfortunately for Rangers and The People, the argument that the police were responsible does not hold water.

It was the same with the trashing of Manchester. Martin Bain, the Rangers Chief Executive, said that the people involved in all the trouble 'don't normally attach themselves to our support',[29] while the Daily Record agreed, saying, 'It was remarkable that almost none of the ringleaders wore club colours or spoke with a Scottish accent. There were, however, many English and Northern Irish accents'.[30]

Essentially, all the blame for what happened in Manchester was shifted onto the police, Manchester Council, Chelsea supporters and whoever was in charge of the big telly. Oh, and Manchester's publicans were castigated as well; it seems that The People are not used to drinking and cannot handle it.[31]

Rangers faced no sanctions from UEFA because all the violence took place away from the stadium.[32] This fortunate turn of events saved Rangers the bother of having to mount an appeal, as they had to do in 1972.[33] The very fact that Rangers appealed UEFA's two-year ban shows that they refused to accept any responsibility.

Rangers, of course, were standing up for their supporters in the *quid-pro-quo* that had been long established. There was, however, more to it than that. The club often required the services of The People to win games or to get matches abandoned when they were losing.

Pitch invasions by The People were a common ploy during Rangers matches. I have read comments about this strategy from newspapers of the 1960s, which, unfortunately, have now disappeared from the internet. The match in Barcelona, however, shows that this strategy was still being employed in the 1970s. There were a few pitch invasions, but the main one came, conveniently, in the dying minutes when Dynamo Moscow had scored two goals and were dominating the match.[34] Arguments that the Rangers supporters thought the match had ended are easily undermined by the fact that The People had already invaded the pitch several times already.

Even when the team was engaged in a friendly match, The People could not stand to see the opposition winning. It was surely no coincidence that Aston Villa were leading 2-0 when 'Sick Saturday' kicked off in 1976. Birmingham suffered because Rangers were losing.

Of course, since they were the Chosen People, they considered themselves the only ones allowed to invade the pitch. At the end of the 1980 Scottish Cup final, the victorious Celtic team went to celebrate with their supporters. Some of the supporters got a bit carried away and climbed over the barrier fence that all big football grounds had in those days. The sight of the Celtic supporters celebrating was too much for The People, who climbed over the barrier to mount an attack. The resulting battle resulted in alcohol being banned at all Scottish matches.

Even then, Rangers tried to blame the Celtic supporters, while those in the press still refuse to point the finger at the real culprits.[35] Nobody wants to ask the simple question as to why The People were still hanging about when their team had lost. Obviously, just as on every other occasion when Rangers lost, The People were spoiling for a fight.

And so, just as in the old days of the Church of Scotland's dominance in Scotland, we had another church claiming that it and its members could do no wrong. Just like back then when members were banished from the congregation for a time, Rangers handed out bans to certain individuals among the support. The new church, however, rarely resorted to the old church's ultimate sanction; banishment for good. And when they did ban anyone for life, the character involved usually just turned up at Ibrox again without anyone bothering. After all, you could not ban one of God's Chosen People from His Church, could you?

6
You Put Your Right Leg In, Your Right Leg Out

While The People's new church was mostly modelled on what they had garnered from Calvinist Presbyterianism, in some ways it went in a completely different direction. To Calvin and Knox, any ceremonial was anathema and reminiscent of Roman Catholicism. The Presbyterian Church was all about preaching and reading the scriptures; nothing else. Priestly vestments were out, prayers that had been learned were out, statues were out, as were chalices, tabernacles, altar boys and, indeed, altars.

Unlike proper Calvinists, however, The People see nothing wrong with ceremonies; neither does their new Church. Since the 1930s, Rangers, and the club that replaced them, has had what is called the *Loving Cup Ceremony*. They all stand around in the boardroom, toast the Queen and then pass a huge mug around filled to the brim with whisky. They all have a solemn sip, as if they are participating in some Eucharistic ceremony.

The idea of a Loving Cup Ceremony appears to come from Freemasonry.[1] The story of its institution at ibrox appears on the new club's website:

> Found within the Ibrox Trophy Room, the Cup is one of only thirty cast from a unique mould to commemorate the coronation in May 1937 of Their Majesties King George VI and Queen Elizabeth.
> The story of how it came into Rangers' possession is part of the club's folklore.
> Identical Loving Cups were presented to the 22 English First Division clubs of the time, with the others going to the British Museum and various organisations.
> Back then, as now, Rangers were recognised as one of the world's great clubs and so it was that they were asked to participate in a special match to raise funds for

the dependents of the miners who lost their lives in the Holditch Colliery Disaster in the Stoke area.
Manager Bill Struth accepted the invitation immediately and Stoke City President, Sir Francis Joseph, presented Rangers with the last of the Loving Cups after the match which finished goalless. His one request was that the vessel should be used in perpetuity to drink to the health of the reigning monarch prior to the club's first home match of every year.
So it is to this day, the New Year toast is celebrated in the Blue Room by the assembled directors and guests of Rangers and their first visiting opponents.[2]

There are a couple of rather embarrassing admissions in among that boastful story. The first is that the Royal Family obviously could not give two hoots for Scotland. Every team in the *English* top division got one of these commemorative mugs. Presumably, the new King did not view himself as the monarch of the United Kingdom. Even more embarrassing, though, is that the club and supporters that have always prided themselves on being the monarch's most loyal servants were completely ignored by their king. They had to stoop to getting a second-hand mug. So much for being 'recognised as one of the world's great clubs'!

As for the ceremony itself, it seems that The People can enter a competition to attend and get a slug from the fancy mug.[3] Having seen some of the scabby, old mouths in the Director's Box at Ibrox and the rotten, broken teeth of The People, you just know that there would be all manner of floaters in that mug. I think I would be demanding first go.

One of The People was worried about a sponsor's whisky being used, saying, 'Great stuff, but I'd be concerned if such an occasion was not sacred from being influenced by sponsorship.' Sacred? Good God! Another calls the big mug the 'great chalice'.[4] Folk had better watch where they are parking in Edinburgh; their suspension will be ruined by John Knox tossing and turning in his grave!

At about the same time each year, there is a commemoration for those that died in the Ibrox Disasters. A wreath is laid, and a solemn prayer is said. Fair enough, although this is a distinctly *un*Protestant thing to do. Calvin and Knox would be furious at such a ceremony; it is as if they are praying for the souls of the departed. And that is not the worst of it. They stand and pray at a *statue*. The statue is of the Patron Saint of Broken Legs – St. John of Greig. And yet when Roman Catholics pray in front of a statue of the Virgin Mary it is called idolatry.

As well as the ceremony at the statue, a minute's silence is sometimes held. This is not held every year and appears to have a twofold purpose. On the one hand, it is a commemoration for those that perished. On the other, however, it is held in the fervent hope that somebody, preferably a Celtic supporter, will cough during it. The People can then express outrage at this disrespect.

One time of the year when they always have a minute's silence is before the match closest to Remembrance Day. This is a part of perhaps the most shocking part of The People's religion: its pantheism. Their worship of the armed forces and, in fact, war, transcends mere jingoism or a concupiscent predilection for men in uniform. One could, quite plausibly, call it the worship of the god Mars.

It seems a strange deity for The People to have; after all, at the first sign of war their team disappears into the shipyards. Probably, though, they view their constant battles with other teams' supporters, the police and even with the general public as warfare of some sort. They certainly seem inordinately proud of their reputation for violence.[5] Then again, they always try to make out as if they are defending themselves from attacks from everybody out there.[6] Apparently, the whole world and his dog hates them.

For many of The People, Remembrance Day has been the highlight of the season for quite a few years now. The players all come onto the park wearing huge poppy transfers on their tops, while The People go wild, waving poppies, poppy banners and trying, and failing, to organise some sort of tifo display. It is often hard for them to concentrate, though, as they have earphones in, with the volume up full, listening in to what Celtic are doing. If they hear so much as a seagull shrieking, it is put down to 'terrorist sympathisers'. On the other hand, if they hear no noise whatsoever during the minute's silence involving Celtic, they claim that Radio Scotland has muted the sound.

When the new club took over at Ibrox, it tried to outdo Rangers in its desperate fawning over the military. Remembrance Day was turned into a fascist circus, with troops abseiling from the roof, march-pasts on the pitch and big guns to signal the minute's silence. Even the top brass in the military was embarrassed at all this, feeling that it was too far from what Remembrance Day is supposed to be about. They, therefore, called a halt to this kind of thing taking place in November.[7]

There was no need to fear, though, since the UK Government decided, in 2006, to institute *Veterans' Day*, which was changed to *Armed Forces Day* in 2009.[8] This takes place on the last Saturday of each June,[9] although organisations are free to host their own events. Nco-Gers, the new club at Ibrox, leapt on this opportunity immediately and have had an *Armed Forces Day* every year since 2013.

The new club boasts too about signing the Armed Forces Covenant,[10] which is a promise by Government, the Armed Forces and various organisations and businesses to support the services' veterans.[11] Strangely, this has not stopped ex-forces men being made homeless and wandering about the streets suffering from mental illness. Then again, perhaps lack of money is the problem, due to certain businesses not paying their taxes.

The People, of course, follow both their old and new clubs in not going too far in their worship of all things military. Mammon, it seems, is further up the pecking order in the pantheon than Mars. Some of them even sell poppies and keep the money themselves.[12] Such entrepreneurial spirit will, no doubt, help them to gain the riches they need to prove that they are members of the Elect.

Along with Mars, indeed, part-and-parcel of the intense love of war and the military, is the worship of Britannia. The idea of any new kind of Britain terrifies The People; their god is the Britannia of old, ruling the waves and all that. They believe those times still exist or, at least, are about to make a comeback.

Bill McMurdo, or *Pastor* Bill McMurdo as he now calls himself, gives this worship of Britannia a spiritual, even a mystical, element:

> It is time for true Christian patriots to stand up and be counted. Don't be ashamed of your nation or your

history. Don't be ashamed to be British. Don't let some idiot tell you that is wrongful pride, either. Make a stand and be a witness to the glorious truth that the greatest empire in world history was the British Empire. And God raised this Empire up, as Queen Victoria, the most powerful ruler in history, faithfully attested to.[13]

You will notice that the 'Chosen People' notion is now extended to all the British; British *Protestants*, that is. Apparently, it was God Himself that told McMurdo all this.[14] (I think He works part-time at the Louden.) Many of The People hate McMurdo, but that is more to do with his opposition to Dave King than any of his religious ramblings. You rarely see them criticise him in this respect.[15]

Another one that provides The People with some kind of structure for their worship of Britannia is Alistair McConnachie, the clown who claims, with arguments that are beyond ridiculous, that the Union between Scotland and England is five thousand years old![16] His contributions to the cause include contending that the British Empire was a great, altruistic enterprise, serving all the peoples of the world.[17]

Of course, McMurdo and McConnachie are both fully in favour of leaving the European Union; Britain cannot fulfil its destiny of leading the world if it is locked into being a minor part of some multi-nation organisation. They, along with all the other Brexit dreamers, think that the natives of Africa, and elsewhere, are just waiting to welcome back 'Bwana'. The People go along with this nonsense as well.

And it goes without saying that this pair, along with The People, were, and are, against Scottish independence. McMurdo, with his usual insanity, thinks that Catholics still vote as a bloc and goes even further:

> It also has to be borne in mind that the nationalist/republican fever in Ireland has largely abated, with polls putting a slight majority of Irish nationalists in Northern Ireland now firmly in favour of staying in the UK – a quite remarkable turnaround from only a couple of decades ago.

As well as this, a growing number of people in the Republic now favour some kind of re-unification with Britain.[18]

This is arrant nonsense, straight from the fevered imagination of McMurdo and nowhere else. It betrays, though, a major concern of The People and why they worship Britannia in the first place. It is all tied up, of course, with the six counties of Ulster known as Northern Ireland.

Remember how, in the Nineteenth Century, many Protestants came to Scotland from Ulster? They maintained their roots as being originally from Scotland and from the North of Ireland. Others came in the early Twentieth Century as well to work in the shipyards. Rangers, especially after John Ure Primrose committed the club to the Unionist cause as well as to Freemasonry, was their natural spiritual home. Primrose even invited Edward Carson to Glasgow.[19]

Eventually, the connection between Rangers and Protestant Unionism became so strong that Protestant Loyalists in the newly-invented state of Northern Ireland began to follow it as well. The Church of The People spread to Northern Ireland, which became, in many ways, a sort of Mecca for The People. Many a Rangers top could be seen all over East Belfast and it came to represent not only a football team, but the Protestant Ascendancy in the Six Counties.

A close connection developed between Belfast club Linfield and Rangers, with each club's supporters also being fans of the other. There was no doubting, however, that Rangers was the main focus; Linfield was effectively just a branch of The People's Church.

The connection with the Protestants of Northern Ireland is the basis for the worship of Britannia. The People know full well that holding the United Kingdom together is the only way to preserve a formal connection. If Scotland were to become independent, Northern Ireland would soon be set adrift; nobody in England or Wales wants anything to do with the place and probably wish their ancestors had never gone near Ireland. That is why Scottish independence is anathema to The People, while the very idea of a united Ireland is enough to give them the vapours.

The People love Britannia but do not have any kind of icon to aid their worship. They could, of course, use an old, pre-decimal penny, which they could stick on the wall beside their beds to pray to. It would kill two birds with one stone, representing Mammon and with a nice picture of Britannia. Putting it on the wall, however, would present a major problem for them; it would mean turning another deity's face toward the wall.

To The People, the British Monarch is the god of Protestantism; a symbol of their superiority over everyone else. The King, or Queen or whatever stands for Protestant and British supremacy; both of which are of the utmost importance to The People. In many ways, it is like the way Rastafarians deified Haile Selassie.[20]

Whenever a new royal baby adds to the taxpayers' burden, The People are overjoyed and sing and chant of their excitement during their team's latest match. Sometimes, they even have one of their half-hearted attempts at a tifo display.

As you might expect, though, when it comes down to it, Mammon wins yet again. The People's old club refused to pay its fair share of taxes, remember, leaving every other taxpayer to pick up the tab for their beloved monarch. The People love having their gods; so long as somebody else pays for them.

7
Walk This Way

Eric Kauffman is Professor of Politics at Birkbeck College, University of London.[1] He is also a prolific writer on right-wing organisations and bigotry.[2] Obviously, his attention has been turned to the Orange Order, both in Northern Ireland and in Scotland. Among several works, he produced a paper showing the decline of the Orange Order in Scotland in the late Twentieth Century.

One of the elements cited is slum clearance, which also seems to be a factor in the post-war decline of the Orange Order in Liverpool.[3] This is certainly a major factor, as anyone that has had the misfortune to attend a party thrown by a certain type of individual can attest. Everything is fine at such a party until it gets to near the end. That is when the Orange records go on and it is your cue to plead tiredness and leave. If you do not get out quickly enough, you will have the dubious pleasure of hearing some of the greatest hits of the Orange Order.

A perennial favourite on these discs is *No Pope of Rome*, which contains the following lines:

> Up a wee narrow close
> Just by Brigton Cross
> Aye it's there the place we call home
> On the twelfth there we join
> To remember The Boyne
> And to pray let's have no Pope of Rome[4]

The slum clearances of the 1960s and 1970s mean that there are hardly any closes, narrow or otherwise, 'just by Brigton Cross' anymore. The folk that used to live there now stay in better housing out in the council estates; some have probably even bought their own houses in more salubrious areas. They still look back with nostalgia, though, to those days of 'community'; even though many of them are too young to remember it.

This element pops up frequently in their songs – 'The bygone days of yore'. The past is everything; those were the good, old days, when Protestants ruled, Catholics knew their place and Britannia ruled the waves. The present is a dark and frightening place, where all the old certainties have disappeared.

One of those certainties was the old, heavy industries, where Orangeism proliferated to make sure that only Protestants got the best jobs. The shipyards, the locomotive industry and even the coal mines have disappeared, meaning that being a member of the Orange Order no longer confers any benefits. The Orange Order is not an attractive option anymore.

To the different Protestant faiths in Scotland, especially the Church of Scotland, the Orange Order has become anathema. The Ecumenical Movement is a huge thing internationally and in Scotland, bringing churches closer together.[5] Encouraging bigots into church services would hardly square with this, which means that Orange Lodges have become *personae non gratae* in most Protestant churches.

And it is not just Ecumenists that want nothing to do with the Orange Order. A leading light in the anti-Ecumenical movement was Pastor Jack Glass, who could, every year, be found demonstrating outside St. Mary's Church in Haddington against the Ecumenical service taking place inside.[6] Glass, however, had no time for the Orange Order because of the licensed social clubs that became associated with the lodges from the 1960s onward.[7]

If Official Scottish Protestantism was turning its back on the Orange Order, it has to be said that the feeling was mutual. The Churches have moved away from the hard-line, right-wing Protestantism espoused by the Orange Order. The Church of Scotland's website has a statement of its faith, which, although it refers to the 'Church's historic Confession of Faith', also says that Christ died on the cross, 'Giving hope and declaring forgiveness of sin, offering healing and wholeness to *all*.' (My italics)[8] Even the Free Church of Scotland, although providing a link to the *Westminster Confession of Faith*, says that 'The gospel message is for everyone'.[9] There was no more *Chosen People*.

That was not all. There are women ministers, gay ministers, the Episcopal Church allowing same-sex weddings in its churches[10] and the Church of Scotland moving in the same direction.[11] With the

Ecumenical Movement putting the tin hat on things, it is hardly surprising that many in the Orange Order view themselves as upholding Protestant traditions, while the churches are drifting dangerously close to Roman Catholicism.

In fact, it often seems as if the only *real* Protestants left are all in Northern Ireland. There is a website called the *Mystery Worshipper*,[12] which operates just like *Mystery Shoppers*, giving reviews of different church services in the UK. It is by no means a representative sample, but the Scottish Presbyterian churches on the site have sermons mostly based on the New Testament, while those in Northern Ireland mostly use the Old Testament. The old, hellfire and brimstone preacher still seems to be in vogue in Northern Ireland.

One such individual is Pastor James McConnell, of the Whitewell Metropolitan Tabernacle. He was the one that ranted about Muslims, calling the Islamic religion 'Satanic'.[13] It would be a rare thing indeed to hear such vicious hatred being preached from a pulpit in Scotland these days. There might, however, be one church where such old-fashioned bigotry could be heard. This is the Glasgow Evangelical Church on Cathedral Square.

When things change in a church, there are always those that are unhappy about it. These people tend to drift off into other churches or even found their own, either official or unofficial. There were those that were upset when the Tridentine Mass disappeared and broke away to continue having Masses in Latin and many High-Church Anglicans converted to Roman Catholicism when their own church allowed female priests. Equally, a church was needed for all the malcontents within Scottish Presbyterianism, unhappy about their churches becoming more modern. Glasgow Evangelical Church provided such a refuge.

The decoration of the church's interior speaks volumes about the congregation's core beliefs. There are stained-glass windows, for example, 'commemorating themes important to the congregation's own particular beliefs – the Bicentenary of Orangeism in Scotland, the Covenanters' Flag and the Solway Martyrs'.[14] And

> Although the congregation is not itself Orange, it occupies a part of the Protestant religious spectrum akin to the Orange Order, sharing similar beliefs, and are mutually supportive of each other.[15]

The lectern, incredibly, is sculpted in the shape of William of Orange.[16] Needless to say, the Orange Order is welcome to hold its services there.

That description of the Glasgow Evangelical Church, saying how it shares 'similar beliefs' to the Orange Order could equally apply to The People. They do not need a church; they already have one at Edmiston Drive. Neither do they need the Orange Order; Rangers and the new club at Ibrox fulfil that function as well. They might turn up at an Orange social club for a drink but, for most of them, the Orange Order is no longer relevant.

Eric Kauffman shows that the Orange Order is comprised of people from lower down the social scale than it used to be.[17] In many ways, though, this means that the drive for respectability has become more pressing. The Order tries to present a face to society of being a non-sectarian organisation, simply existing to promote and 'defend' Protestantism. To this end it actively discourages any links to Loyalist paramilitary groups; on the surface, at any rate.

This respectability, however, does not appeal to The People; nobody is telling them what to do. If they want to sing songs praising the UVF, or even raise funds for terrorist organisations, then they are going to do it, no matter what anyone thinks or says. Their lodge-cum-church is their own affair and they have no great interest in respectability, especially other people's interpretation of it.

That, of course, never stops The People following behind an Orange Walk, exhibiting that strange gait they have, suggestive of suffering from rickets, or punching the air one fist at a time. They are not interested in the ones marching in bowler hats and white gloves, however; it is the bands they want to follow. And the more bigoted the tunes the bands play, the better they like it.

It is a strange situation that exists regarding Orange Walks; bands are separate entities, unaffiliated to any lodge. Without the bands, there would be no spectacle to an Orange Walk, so the lodges need the bands. At the same time, though, they view the bands with the utmost distaste.[18] It seems that, quite often, the behaviour of the bands, especially those from Scotland, is unbecoming to the dignity of the Orange Order.[19]

In my book *Up to Our Knees*, which looked at anti-Catholic bigotry in Scotland, I told the story of a boy I taught, who always turned up to school dressed in a Rangers waterproof jacket, a Rangers bag, a

Rangers pencil case etc. He had no interest in football whatsoever, could not tell you what the score had been at the weekend or even name one Rangers player. I got one thing wrong in my telling; I said that his family were involved with the local Orange *Lodge*, but it was a *band* they were, and are, in. The reason why the boy had so much Rangers merchandise was simply because Orange merchandise does not exist.[20]

Speaking about the parades in Northern Ireland, T.G. Fraser, of the University of Ulster, says,

> Pipe bands and brass bands have long disappeared from the Belfast parade, though the former are still well represented in certain country areas. Some well established flute and accordion bands have held their position and maintain a high musical standard, but the tone of parades has increasingly been set by the so-called 'blood and thunder' flute bands.[21]

This has come about because the parades have become 'more oppositional in tone'[22] since The Troubles. Scotland appears to have gone down the same route. I cannot say that I remember ever seeing pipe bands and brass bands at Orange Walks before The Troubles; but there certainly were plenty of accordion bands. Maybe it is just that fashion has changed; accordions were ubiquitous in the 1960s and no party was complete without a drunk uncle playing one while everybody sang along. Then again, there has developed a definite martial air around Orange bands. Although, they call themselves 'flute bands', they actually play military fifes; there are no Ian Andersons among them.

If the Orange Order has been obsessed with seeking respectability, the flute bands most decidedly have not. It often seems as if loudness takes precedence over musical ability with these bands. That lad I taught was, and still is, a fifer, even though, to him, a quaver was just a type of crisp. Presumably, he, and the rest of the none-too-bright individuals I taught that are in his band, learned to play by ear.

Most normal bands, like pipe bands and brass bands, are led by a Drum Major. This character walks in front in a dignified manner, holding a large mace, which he moves rhythmically to set the beat that the band follows. Orange bands, however, have somebody in front, twirling a baton like a majorette. Round his shoulders and up in the air goes the 'stick'; anybody in the band trying to follow a beat set by this clown would be in serious trouble.

Instead, the beat is set by a drum. The bands scour the earth for the dimmest clods they can find to play this particular instrument; if you can call what they do 'playing'. Essentially, they beat hell out of the drum like a two-year-old banging a biscuit tin with two spoons. And, just like the 'stick man', they dance around all over the place. Of course, a normal drum could not take this kind of treatment, so they have to use a reinforced, moron-proof instrument called a 'Lambeg'.

It is quite a ridiculous-looking sight of a July morning, viewing a group of smug, self-satisfied men and women, walking proudly beneath banners and wearing their sashes, white gloves etc., followed by a clown throwing a stick about, leading a band of fifers, among whom a big heid-the-baw batters a drum as if his life depended on it. This lot, in turn, are followed by a crowd of manky drunks, dressed in old, unwashed Rangers tops. It is hardly an edifying spectacle.

It is difficult to decide which group is the most ludicrous. The old bigots march along, trying their best to look dignified while the circus follows behind. They usually end up at Glasgow Green, where, presumably, the ones from the lodges go off somewhere else; possibly to an open-air service or to their special church on Cathedral Square. The bandsmen and The People, meanwhile, get pissed and fight with each other.

Very few of The People join the Orange Order anymore; the Order tries to pretend that it is not a sectarian organisation, while The People wear their bigotry on their sleeves. Their only real interest in Orangeism, apart from looking back to the good old days, is in the bands. The Orange bands, for their part, are more aligned with The People than they are with the lodges. The Order would like the bands to play hymns, while The People want *No Pope of Rome* and the *Famine Song*. The fact that the bands play The People's choice shows whose side they are on.

Some of The People join Orange bands, while the bandsmen have a strong affinity with Rangers and the new Ibrox club. In fact, as we saw with my old pupil, Rangers and Orangeism, as represented by the bands, have long been so close that affinity with one generally means affinity with the other. All the good, old, anti-Catholic and anti-Irish songs are belted out at Ibrox, displaying The People's love for the Orange Order of old. Only they and the Orange bands keep the old traditions alive; in Scotland, at any rate.

Rangers, ostensibly at least, tried to break with this sectarianism within its support, banning *Simply the Best* because of the add-ons and trying to outlaw the *Billy Boys*. This, however, was just window dressing and there is no record of anyone every having been banned from Ibrox for bigoted singing or chanting. Besides, the club's own anthems, which it blares over the loudspeakers, *Follow Follow* and *There's Not a Team Like the Glasgow Rangers*, betray anti-Irish and anti-Celtic FC sentiments.

Since the advent of the new club at Ibrox, sectarian bigotry has been positively encouraged. A siege mentality has been developed, pretending that the club has been badly treated. It suits the ones in charge to foster the absurd story that bigotry *against* the club has caused all its problems. This suits the atavistic paranoia of The People, who can guard *Derry's Walls* all over again. More about this later.

As with any such organisation, The People's church-cum-lodge has an inner circle, albeit a self-appointed one. This close-knit bunch makes it its business to be a mouthpiece for The People and many of them seem to be perfectly happy about this. This group lets us all have a peek inside the minds of The People and how they view themselves.

The *Vanguard Bears* website shows the legend, 'Defending our traditions'.[23] Although the website constantly talks about Protestantism, there could be nothing more *un*Protestant than this short statement. Protestantism, as we saw earlier, was all about sweeping aside traditions; all that mattered was what it said in the Bible. The Catholic Church relied on tradition, as well as the Bible, which Reformers claimed was totally wrong. Traditions like believing in Purgatory, having statues in churches etc. were deemed to be no longer relevant as they were not in the Bible.

Unfortunately, the Bible can often be a rather unreliable source for doctrine, as many parts contradict other parts. For example, the Gospels tell us to love our neighbour, no matter what, while St. Paul's letters are very selective about whom we should love and often appear to be full of hate. It was the latter, along with the Old Testament, that Protestants of old concentrated on, ignoring the Gospels.

Give Scottish Protestantism its due; it has proven to be still dynamic and not hidebound by tradition. The Church of Scotland, especially, has simply looked again at the Bible and realised that it was relying on the wrong bits. It now mostly uses the Gospels; tradition does not come into it.

And yet, tradition is everything to The People, their new club and the *Vanguard Bears*. There is some crossover here with the Orange Order, especially with that in Northern Ireland. As the *Vanguard Bears* describe themselves:

> Established in 2007, Vanguard Bears are a group of Loyalist & Unionist Rangers supporters, whose aims are to ensure that the good standing and unionist tradition of THE quintessential British Club is maintained, and to support the Protestant Unionist Loyalist community in Scotland, Ulster and beyond. Our motto "Defending Our Traditions" refers to this.[24]

And what are those 'traditions' that the *Vanguard Bears* seek to 'defend'? Well, perceived attacks on Rangers and the new club have been paramount, but they also look to defend Orange Walks from 'Republican filth across Scotland and Ulster'.[25] Charming. In fact, they see enemies everywhere, all looking to destroy the new Ibrox club, and the 'PUL community'. But, what the hell *is* the PUL community?

Well, the 'Unionist' bit is easily explained; it is about the terror of the UK breaking up and Northern Ireland being cast adrift, or worse, being reunited with the rest of Ireland. The term 'Loyalist' is tied up with Northern Ireland as well and refers to all the royalty-worshippers there, among The People and in the Orange Order in Scotland. Such a simple explanation, however, does not work for the term 'Protestant'.

As we have already seen, The People and the Scottish Protestant churches parted company a long time ago, so the term 'Protestant' obviously means something different to each of these groupings. Since the Protestant religions have moved on into the Twenty-First Century, The People and their ilk have stopped speaking about the Protestant faith practically altogether. What they speak of now is *culture*; either PUL culture or, more generally, Protestant culture.

8
Culture Shock

In Scotland, different classes have different pastimes. The upper-class Torquhils, Ossians, Peregrines, Eleanors and Ionas attend numerous 'reeling parties',[1] watch Highland Games and go around shooting anything that moves. You will not see a satellite dish attached to any of their castles; watching television is so *infra dig*! There are various other pastimes or hobbies that these people indulge in; they are brought up to know which are acceptable and which are not. If you need to ask, then you are *not* one of them, no matter how much money you have.

The middle classes, meanwhile, are all about dinner parties, going to the theatre and getting your children into the best schools. Skiing holidays are an absolute must, as is reading the right books and watching the right TV programmes. Murrayfield is the place to go if you want to watch sport; they all played rugby at school, after all. Dressing as if you do your clothes shopping at jumble sales is *de rigueur*, even though closer examination betrays how expensive the clothing really is. This is part of the pretence of being left-wing or liberal, while secretly voting Tory.

Then we have the working classes, who enjoy a drink, watch too much TV, watch football, bet on the horses, go to bingo and aspire to having at least one foreign holiday a year. Sometimes they can be as obsessed with respectability as anyone from the middle classes, at other times, the self-same folk do not care about respectability at all. It all depends on the circumstances. And, just like the upper classes, if you have to ask what is acceptable and when, then you do not belong.

These collective pastimes are called *cultures*: upper-class culture, middle-class culture, working-class culture. There are all sorts of cultures, about which folk make sweeping generalisations. There is youth culture, for example, which implies that everybody young does the exact same things. The same applies when people talk about a country's culture; not everybody in that country joins in or agrees with it. Bullfighting, for example, is often said to be a part of Spanish culture; it is pretty much a minority that enjoys it, though, and there are many in Spain that want it banned.

The biggest generalisation, however, is when people speak of a religion's culture. Many folk currently do this with Islam. You will hear them going on about how Muslims treat their women and how those women are second-class citizens. Saudi Arabia, however, where women *are* treated as second-class, is vastly different from Pakistan, which has even had a female prime minister. It is the same with female genital mutilation, which really only happens in some African countries. It is *tribal* culture, rather than religious.

The People, though, think that religious culture is a real thing and speak of *Protestant* culture. This, of course, is absolute nonsense and assumes that this 'culture' cuts across class boundaries; it most decidedly does not. Upper-class and middle-class Protestants would not be seen dead following an Orange band or at a football match, singing bigoted songs. They might agree with the sentiments, but it would not be the done thing to be *seen* to agree. Essentially, this 'culture' is a working-class thing.

So, what sets The People's 'culture' apart from ordinary, working-class culture? Not much. They like a bevvy, the same as everybody else, they watch the same television programmes, Mrs. People probably enjoys the bingo and the whole family will be off to Tenerife or Turkey for their holidays. There is only one thing that sets them apart: hatred.

All the marching round the streets of Glasgow and Belfast and all the singing and chanting at Ibrox is about hatred of Catholics and the Irish. As we saw already, the Protestant churches in Scotland do not harbour such hatred anymore. There might be some among the congregation that would like a return to the old days and old ways, but they tend to keep their mouths shut. For The People, Protestantism is no longer their religion; it is just an excuse to hate Catholics, especially Irish Catholics. That is their 'culture'; hating folk.

As usual, the *Vanguard Bears* give us an insight into how The People view things. To them, it is everybody else that is doing the hating. Incredibly, they try to compare Orange Walks to religious festivals around the world and to historical reconstructions in Spain.

> In the Balearics, you have Es Firo in Majorca, celebrating "Moors v Christians" which is essentially a celebration of The Roman Catholic Church driving Islam out of their Island. No one bats an eyelid.[2]

Actually, people do more than bat an eyelid and many of the offensive, anti-Islamic elements of these festivals have been toned down, much to the chagrin of right-wing groups.[3] It was probably not the best example for *Vanguard Bears* to use.

Even more ridiculous are the claims about 'hate filled anti-English or anti-Semitic marches dressed up as pro-Palestine or pro separation marches'.[4] They say this without a hint of irony, as if they honestly believe what they are saying.

We are all familiar with the *bonefires* throughout Northern Ireland on 11th July each year, where representations of Loyalists' 'enemies' are burnt. Tragically, and rather frighteningly, this happens at so-called children's fun days![5] The effigies, posters and other items on the *bonefires* are mostly what you would expect: Irish flags, pictures of Sinn Fein politicians etc. but that is not the end of it. Celtic FC features prominently, as do racist insults aimed at Celtic players and, more recently, Muslims.[6] What was it *Vanguard Bears* were saying about hate-filled?

The People, of course, support all these expressions of hatred in Northern Ireland, in fact, it is more than that; those Northern-Irish Loyalists are members of The People as well. Many of them travel to Ibrox frequently, just as the Scottish contingent of The People go to Northern Ireland once or twice a year, in what might be termed a 'cultural' exchange.

Connal Parr, of Northumbria University, tries to argue against what he calls '…the fallacy that the Protestant working class in Northern Ireland has no culture but the Orange Order and Rangers F.C.'.[7] Unfortunately for his thesis, he misses the whole point of what constitutes culture.

In his book *Inventing the Myth: Political Passions and the Ulster Protestant Imagination*, Parr looks at writers and playwrights that come from a Northern-Irish, Protestant, working-class background. Just because someone comes from such a background, however, does not mean that they are representative of that background's culture. In fact, most people from a working-class background that make it big in the world of arts and literature only do so because they appeal to the middle classes.

Would Irvine Welsh, for example, even have been published if there was not a ready-made, middle-class audience out there, keen to read what they think life is like in council schemes? And then there is Jimmy Boyle, whose twisted bits of metal and stone are viewed as art by the middle classes. Far from being rehabilitated, Boyle revels in his unsavoury past, while his middle-class admirers are prepared to accept that he was simply a product of his environment. Nobody in their right mind would accept that either Welsh or Boyle are representative of Scottish, working-class culture.

Of course, that is not to say that working-class people cannot enjoy the same things as middle-class folk; the truth is, though, that many of them do not want to. No doubt there were working-class Protestants that read the books or watched the plays listed by Connal Parr but, in the main, they would be the preserve of the middle classes.

When I was at university, I joined an Anarchist group for a laugh. They tended to be studying English Literature Philosophy and Politics, which struck me as pretty useless if they were serious about bringing down society. Computing would surely have been better as they could have learned how to hack into the Capitalists' computer systems. Anyway, they are probably all working for those self-same capitalists these days.

Some local punks came along to the meetings and they seemed to have far more experience of such groups than the vegetarian, hippy students. One group they told us about was a bunch of middle-class Anarcho-Communists. This lot used to start every meeting by watching *Coronation Street*. Laughable as this might seem, the group could do a lot worse. They were not watching Coronation Street to learn how the working classes lived, but to share in their culture.

Working-class culture in Scotland has changed dramatically since the 1960s. In Glasgow in the early 1960s, there were still plenty of cinemas, dance-halls and pubs in the centre of Glasgow. Theatres, like the Metropole, had variety shows with Andy Stewart, the Alexander Brothers etc. and often played to packed houses. There were all-purpose halls that local folk could use for meetings, classes, board games etc. By the 1970s, this had all disappeared.

Slum clearances and the moving of people out to suburban council schemes, as we saw in the last chapter, had a great effect on the Orange Order, but it also affected working-class culture. Pubs were few and far between, and non-existent in the case of Castlemilk, leading to folk drinking at home rather than going out. This happened to be cheaper as well. There were Community Centres, but these tended to focus on the two extremes of youth and elderly. They were not like the all-purpose halls of old.

Going to the theatre used to involve a short tram-ride or even a short walk, but now you would have to sit on a bus for up to an hour to get there. People coming home from work could hardly face such a two-way journey, especially since they had probably travelled a long way from their place of work out to the council scheme. Besides, what was the point of going away into town to see Stanley Baxter, Lex McLean or Andy Stewart when you could watch them on the telly?

More and more, working-class entertainment, culture, that is, has become an individual or family affair. Collective forms of entertainment have all but died out; even the bingo halls are giving way to internet gaming rooms. In fact, the only collective working-class entertainment left is football spectating. Even that, though, has, in many cases, been priced beyond the pocket of working-class people. It is hardly surprising that the move toward individual entertainment is affecting football as well. More people watch football on Sky Sports or BT Sports than they do at stadia.

But, still, plenty of folk manage to get season tickets and get out to support their team, even travelling to away matches in Europe. To the Northern-Irish contingent of The People, every game is an away match, except when their team turns up to play a friendly at Windsor Park. In spite of the high unemployment that has existed in the Six Counties for decades, the ferries to Scotland still tend to be packed.

The changes in working-class culture have affected Northern Ireland as well. Slum clearance, however, did not have quite the same effect on the Orange Order that it had in Scotland. In Belfast, for example, there were fears that whole communities would be destroyed, while politicians worried about their constituents disappearing.[8] Sectarian housing policies and the Troubles combined, though, to cause the new housing estates to be divided along religious lines.[9] Within this situation, the Orange Order survived intact; in fact, it thrived.

Again, it has to be stressed that not all of those that subscribe to Orangeism are members of the Order. There are divers Loyalist groups in Northern Ireland, both paramilitary and political. The Order banned its members from joining terrorist organisations but there are definitely links between them. Besides, just as in Scotland, every Orange Walk is cheered on and followed by non-affiliated hangers-on. In terms of belief, these characters are no different from the bowler-hatted ones in the middle of the street.

To The People in Northern Ireland, the idea of having a 'Protestant Culture' is far more vital than it is in Scotland. Democratic Unionist Party politician Nelson McCausland explains what the problem is. He talks of a Catholic school in Belfast, where

> ...the children are immersed in the Irish Gaelic culture of that community, which it describes as "their culture", with Gaelic games, Irish language, Irish song, Irish dancing, Irish traditional music, Irish folklore and Irish language signage.[10]

The way McCausland disparagingly puts inverted commas around the phrase 'their culture' speaks volumes about his, and others' agenda. They imagine that Northern-Irish *Catholics* have a culture, so *Protestants* need to have one as well. That *Catholic* culture, however, is an *Irish* one, shared throughout the island. Attempts to promote some kind of separate, *Protestant* 'culture' have been dismal failures.

Journalist and broadcaster Malachi O'Doherty, while pursuing a completely different agenda, inadvertently pinpoints what the problem is. He writes, 'A persistent failure by republicans here to understand Northern Ireland Protestants is rooted in the false assumption that they are all the same.'[11]

In fact, it is the Protestants themselves that are guilty of this. The so-called Protestant Unionist Loyalist (PUL) community is, in fact, not really a 'community' at all. As the journalist Denis Murray put it, talking of the civil-rights movement of the 1960s,

> The Catholic-nationalist minority had decided it would no longer accept second-class citizenship. There are elements of the Protestant population which find this "uppity" aspiration of Catholics too much to bear to this day. It finds its expression in spurious claims of "the erosion of Protestant culture", by which they really mean the end of unionist-Protestant supremacy.[12]

The state of Northern Ireland was an artificial construct, as was the whole idea of the Protestant Ascendancy. As such, maintaining this ascendancy and ensuring the continuance of Northern Ireland was all the Protestants had in common. As we saw in Chapter 2, Presbyterians and other Nonconformists were treated not much differently from Catholics, even at the end of the Eighteenth Century. The shared history of Ulster Protestants did not come until later; much later.

Despite all the nonsense about British Israelism and the Cruthins,[13] the Protestants of Northern Ireland do not have a collective history that goes further back than the Nineteenth Century. In fact, the very term 'Protestant' shows how artificial the whole business is.

Ask anybody out in the real world what their religion is and they will answer Catholic, Church of England, Church of Scotland, Free Church, Episcopalian, Methodist etc. We are talking about *real* Christians here, though; people that actually go to church of a Sunday. Hardly anyone would describe themselves as a 'Protestant'; they know there is no such thing as the *Protestant Church* and, besides, they view their own religion as being distinct from that of others.

The whole concept of describing oneself as a 'Protestant' was sparked by Irish Nationalism. The 'Home Rule is Rome Rule' spiel started in the 1880s, when Gladstone tried to push through Irish Home Rule at Westminster. This caused different denominations to band together as 'Protestants' to fight the possible future of living in a 'Catholic' Ireland. Protestants came together even more in the early Twentieth Century with the rise of Sinn Fein. Essentially, the term 'Protestant' simply came to mean 'Non-Catholic'.

Like almost everywhere in Europe, church attendance in Northern Ireland has fallen drastically since the Second World War.[14] That, however, has not stopped people from still calling themselves 'Protestants'. Many such people have never seen the inside of a church and, in fact, the only way religion enters their lives is in their hatred of Catholics. Protestantism is no longer a religion; it is more a state of mind.

The decline in religiosity among so-called Protestants is why there is so much talk of 'culture'; nobody is quite sure how to describe them or their beliefs anymore. Meanwhile, the equivalent drop in religiosity among the Nationalists has left the Unionists facing an existential dilemma. In fact, more than that, it is an identity crisis.

Unionism is so necessarily wrapped up in Protestantism and Orangeism that it is hardly tailored to appeal to Catholics. Nationalist Republicanism, on the other hand, left behind any religious associations long ago. This means that the idea of a united Ireland is open to anyone and everyone. Even immigrants to Northern Ireland, while not necessarily supporting a united Ireland, do not see any reason to oppose it.[15]

The Irish Republic, meanwhile, has moved on and is becoming a much more secular society. The Catholic Church no longer has the power and influence it once had and Ireland has already become, in many ways, much more open and liberal than Northern Ireland. The insistence of the Unionists in Northern Ireland that they are defending their 'freedoms' against the 'tyranny' of Rome is no longer relevant and appears rather ridiculous.

Theologian John Roberts, says that, 'Being "Protestant" is so important that the label continues, with the religion to justify and support this identity, and subsequently, the need for Northern Ireland.'[16] Roberts does not explicitly state it, but his thesis implies that the whole reason for the existence of Northern Ireland, with it being a part of the UK, relies on a circular argument. There needs to be a Northern Ireland to maintain a confident, visible Protestantism, while a confident, visible Protestantism is essential for the existence of Northern Ireland. According to Roberts,

> The politics of Paisley and other Unionists with their evangelical Protestant nature are "ultimately the only viable [identity] for defending the continued social and

cultural autonomy and dominance of Ulster Loyalists" who use religion to create a difference between them and Catholics, and ultimately any other group which has resulted not only in historical sectarian clashes, but also an increase in racist and xenophobic attacks on migrant communities in Northern Ireland.[17]

And therein lies a huge problem with The People, both in Northern Ireland and in Scotland. Their blinkered view of the world and paranoid nature makes them easy prey for any right-wing racist that is looking for folk to manipulate. All he needs to do is don a Rangers top and pay lip service to Northern-Irish Unionism. The People will then follow like sheep.

As far back as the 1980s, recruiters for the National Front and then the British National Party were a common sight at Ibrox stadium. Many of these right-wing thugs and hooligans had links with Ulster Loyalist groups,[18] making them highly attractive to The People, both in Scotland and Northern Ireland. Strangely, though, The People always deny that they are involved with fascism or Nazism. To their minds, they cannot possibly be; both fascism and Nazism are *Catholic* things. After all, Adolf Hitler, Benito Mussolini and Francisco Franco were all Catholics, were they not?

This is a common argument and there is no denying that Mussolini, and certainly Franco, never abandoned their Catholic faith. Hitler, though, definitely left his Catholic upbringing far behind him. The People, however, always argue that Catholicism stays with one for life. This is easily countered by pointing out that John Knox was a Catholic as well.

In fact, the links between Ulster Loyalists and fascist groups are long-standing. Ian Paisley, in the 1960s, went out of his way to make common cause with white supremacists in the USA. His newspaper spoke out against African-American civil rights leaders and Paisley himself accepted an honorary doctorate from a racially-segregated university.[19] The ties have been there ever since, which has led to some bizarre behaviour among The People in Northern Ireland.

White supremacist organisations in America have other hate figures than simply black people; they hate Jews as well.[20] These nutjobs believe that black people are intellectually inferior to whites, so they are obviously the puppets of powerful Jews. In this respect,

American fascists and Nazis hate Jews far more than they hate black people. They believe that if Jews are removed from the equation, then blacks will become again the subservient creatures they are supposed to be!

Throughout Northern Ireland, especially on the 11th July 'Bonefire Night', Loyalists show their affiliation with the 'Good Ol' Boys' of the Ku Klux Klan etc. by flying Confederate flags. They also display swastikas to prove how much they love their American friends. Curiously, and with not a hint of irony, alongside these racist emblems can be seen the flag of Israel.

Such are the workings of the minds of The People. What they call 'culture' is hatred, nothing more; although they are often confused about whom it is they are supposed to hate. The simple guide they use is if Irish Republicans, Catholics or Celtic supporters are for it, then they are against it, and vice-versa. Irish Republicans and Celtic supporters are on the side of the beleaguered Palestinians, so The People hate them and fly the flag of Israel to show this. They are nothing if not a confused bunch.

Sometimes, The People like to show their affinity with their brothers in the USA by making Nazi salutes. They even did this when their team was playing in Israel.[21] Their rather pathetic excuse was that they were making 'Red Hand' salutes. This was a complete invention, and nobody had ever heard of such a thing. They have stuck to this story ever since, even though they are as aware of how nonsensical it is as much as everybody else.

This, then, is the 'culture' that the likes of the *Vanguard Bears* want to protect. It is not a culture at all, but neither is it a religion. Protestantism is an umbrella term for a multitude of different churches, some of which can be mutually antagonistic. That, and the decline in religiosity, leaves Protestantism as nothing but an artificial, political construct to keep a certain section of the population away from the levers of power.

When the political situation changed, and Catholics were allowed to participate in the running of the artificial state, all the 'Protestants' were left with was their hatred. That is something, it appears, that they are extremely reluctant to let go of.

9
Boys Keep Swinging

Women, in general, have fared pretty badly throughout history. In the ancient world, they were, for the most part, considered nothing more than possessions, not much better than slaves. Yes, they worshipped goddesses, but even those goddesses tended to be representations of women as objects of sexuality and fertility. Society was run by men and a woman was just there to fulfil a man's needs, whether as a lover, a mother or an old crone preparing his body for burial.

Judaism was not much better as monotheism meant a male God, with no room for goddesses. Some point to the preponderance of females in the Old Testament as evidence that women played an important part in Judaism, but, in fact, that is not the case. The books of the Old Testament are full of stories of women as temptresses – Eve; objects of lust – Bathsheba; and of doting mothers – Rebecca. The story of Lot showed that even daughters were just there to bear one's children, in the absence of other women.

The early Christian Church seems to have had an abundance of women in it, some of whom were leaders of their communities. It is possible that women even held positions of authority, such as deacons or even priests.[1] St. Paul spoke of some of these women although, as we have seen, he was not too happy about women being in charge.

Once Christianity became the state religion, the women were unceremoniously thrown out of positions of authority and, no doubt, instructed to go home and get the dinner on. Only men could lead the Church and only men could lead church services. Women had been put firmly back in their place.

As the centuries wore on, however, the worship of the Virgin Mary grew in the Catholic Church, meaning that women could no longer be seen as worthless. Women set up their own orders and led them, without interference from men; many of them ended up being proclaimed saints. It is important, though, not to overstate this female independence and leadership within the Church; when it came right down to it, men were in charge.

It is true, nonetheless, that the practice in the Catholic Church of praying to saints to intercede with God made no distinction between male and female saints. And the most important intermediary to pray to was Christ's mother, the Virgin Mary. Women might have been subordinate to men in the Church, but the preponderance of female saints obviously helped to give them some sense of worth.

The Reformation swept all the saints, including the Virgin Mary, aside. Now, it was just God; a male God, with no female involvement at all. Women were back to square one. Protestants 'recognized (sic) and celebrated the value of women's status as wives and mothers',[2] but that was it. Women were no longer spiritual beings that could lead religious orders or intercede with God on people's behalf.

Contemporary notions of how human reproduction worked hardly helped. Women were seen as merely vessels, in which men's seed developed. To many Reformers, this was the reason for 'downgrading' the Virgin Mary to a role of practically no importance whatsoever. Women in general, however, were also 'downgraded' accordingly.

How women were seen by the Reformers is summed up by John Knox in his essay, *The First Blast of the Trumpet Against the Monstrous Regiment of Women*:

> I except such as God, by singular privilege, and for certain causes known only to himself, has exempted from the common rank of women, and do speak of women as nature and experience do this day declare them. Nature, I say, does paint them forth to be weak, frail, impatient, feeble, and foolish; and experience has declared them to be inconstant, variable, cruel, lacking the spirit of counsel and regiment. And these notable faults have men in all ages espied in that kind, for the which not only they have removed women from rule and authority, but also some have thought that men subject to the counsel or empire of their wives were unworthy of public office.[3]

Strangely, given how women were viewed by the Reformers (who were all male), many women flocked to the new religion. Certainly, there were those women that were able to make up their own minds; educated women, like nuns. A prime example was the nun that became the wife of Martin Luther, Katharina von Bora. Other, less educated women, who made up the majority, were no doubt caught up in the Reformers' declarations of 'freedom'. There is, though, another explanation as to why women were so keen to get involved in the Reformation.

If one were to go to a service of the Church of Jesus Christ of Latter-Day Saints, the Mormons, one would be struck by how women vastly outnumber men in the congregation. There is no great mystery to this; it is simply that most people are introduced to the Mormon Church by young, male missionaries knocking on their door. I was once a member of this church and the women I encountered there were widows, divorcees, stuck in unhappy marriages or young women with self-esteem issues. It was pretty obvious that they were all there because of the young, clean-cut Americans that had been visiting their homes. My mother, who dragged my brothers and me along, was no exception. One of the reasons why I left the church was because, once I turned sixteen, some of the middle-aged women began to look at me in the same way they did those American missionaries. I was scared half to death!

This sort of thing happened back during the Reformation as well. John Knox, for instance, was hugely popular with women. Looking at drawings, paintings and prints of the Reformers, it has to be said that they do not strike one as sexually attractive individuals. Whatever we might thing, however, the fact is that women *did* find them sexually attractive. What was their secret? Believe it or not, the answer is – beards!

In modern times, we are used to men trying to make themselves attractive to the opposite sex by emulating celebrities. In the early 1970s, women used to swoon over the television character, *Jason King*. This engendered a plethora of clones, all dressed in three-piece suits, safari jackets and Zapata moustaches. Nowadays, in the second decade of the 21st Century, the sartorial role model seems to be *Captain Birdseye*, with young men sporting beards left, right and centre. There are some interesting theories about why this hirsuteness has become so fashionable.

Apparently, women are not too keen on beards,[4] although this has not stopped their proliferation. A psychoanalyst theorises that men are going through something of a crisis of identity, caused, in part, by the erosion of demarcated gender roles and the rise of powerful women.[5] In this scenario, the beard is a phallic symbol. This was the case during the Reformation as well.

It cannot escape anyone's notice that all of the Reformers sported beards; even Luther grew one. Speculation about why tends to concentrate on them trying to look like Old-Testament prophets or even that it was an anti-Catholic statement. Catholic clergy were all clean-shaven.[6] In fact, this only highlights the use of beards as phallic symbols and signs of manliness; Roman Catholic clergy were celibate, Reformed clergy were decidedly not. The beard, then, was a sign of virility; the bigger the beard, the bigger the…er…virility.

In a sense, therefore, the Reformers were advertising their availability to women. Many women, both then and now, can find themselves attracted to a member of the Roman Catholic clergy; they know, however, that, for the most part, their passion is one-sided and doomed from the start. It must have been intoxicating for women to be confronted by the likes of Knox, a powerful leader of the new church, with his big beard dangling provocatively in front of them. It goes without saying that the Reformers took full advantage of their sexual allure to promote their cause.

As we have seen (Chapter 2), women tended to be punished for sinfulness far more than men in Protestant Scotland. It was as if women were to blame for all the world's evils and the Church's reliance on the Old Testament would have had the example of Eve to the forefront of its teaching. Women were often viewed as instruments of the Devil, who could only be saved if they played their allotted role as wives and mothers. This hypocrisy became magnified in Victorian times, with Scotland succumbing to English mores as part of the United Kingdom.

Everybody is probably familiar with the *Every Sperm Is Sacred* part of the film *Monty Python's Meaning of Life*. Not only does this parody Roman Catholic attitudes to birth control, it also pokes fun at those of Protestants. The Protestant husband boasts about how he can use condoms, while his obviously frustrated wife demands to know why he does not. Both these characterisations are stereotypes, of course, but they do point to mindsets with which we are all familiar.

Towards the end of the Victorian period, the birth rate declined across Europe and across class boundaries.[7] It used to be believed, and still is in some quarters, that this was due to the availability of rubber condoms. I remember looking into this myself at university and finding that, although middle-class people could have used the new type of condoms, they were beyond the financial reach of ordinary, working-class folk. My conclusion was that it was abstinence, rather than barrier methods of birth control, that was responsible for the falling birth rate.

Other historians have investigated the phenomenon in far more depth than I did but reached roughly the same conclusion. It seems that people were waiting longer to get married and were spacing their children, rather than churning them out as they did in the middle of the century.[8] Once married, couples were practising abstinence from full sexual intercourse; of course, there were other things they could have done. These do not have to be detailed; use your imagination!

In the mid-Nineteenth Century, upper- and middle-class men used prostitutes quite frequently; the sheer numbers of prostitutes of all types in Britain in that period is testament to this. Those men, however, still went home and fathered huge families. No doubt there were plenty of men using prostitutes in the late Victorian period (although the fear of venereal diseases and legislation against having sex with those under the age of sixteen helped dampen down the practice) but now, at home, they were having smaller families. Obviously, something radical had happened to change attitudes.

In the early Victorian period, infant mortality was extremely high. That was the reason why they had big families; there was every chance that some of a couple's children would die before they reached adulthood. It was not unknown for two or more children, especially boys, to be given the same first name, to make sure that name survived. The infant mortality rate declined in the late Nineteenth Century with better understanding and prevention of diseases; now, large families were no longer a requirement.

With the fear of children dying almost removed, economic considerations took over. The rise of wages in real terms toward the end of the Nineteenth Century[9] would have led to a measure of aspiration among the working classes. This was the period when working-class people started to take up leisure pursuits, like going to the coast for the day. A large family would have been detrimental to these aspirations; as would marrying too young. Even among working-class women it was expected that, once they were married, they should give up their job. Putting off marriage meant two people working and saving until they were ready to set up house.

Once married, however, it was most definitely abstinence that was used as birth control. That frustrated woman in the *Monty Python* film was not a figment of their imagination. Many middle-class women in Victorian times had to go to their doctors to seek relief from 'hysteria'. Essentially, this was sexual frustration and was 'treated' by masturbation. Electric vibrators were invented to save wear and tear on doctors' hands; testament to the many female patients each medic had to 'treat' every day.[10] Presumably, working-class women were too busy to worry about 'hysteria'; they had no servants to cook and clean for them.

We saw earlier (Chapter 4) how the Scottish Protestant underclass was practically disowned by its own church. Even the Orange Order wanted nothing to do with the lower classes if it could help it. The Scottish Protestant underclass, however, still saw itself as *Protestant*, so its members did what they always did; they followed the lead of their social betters.

As Britain moved into the Twentieth Century, it carried over the mores of the Nineteenth Century with it. In fact, most historians agree that the 'Nineteenth Century' as a concept did not end until the First World War blasted it out of existence. In the first decade or so of the new century, Victorian values were still to the fore.

The two big issues in Britain in the pre-war years were Irish Home Rule and women's suffrage. The latter was mostly the concern of upper- and middle-class women; any working-class women involved were just being used in the same way as working-class men were in the run-up to the 1832 extension of the franchise. This was proven when the vote was only given to middle-class women over the age of thirty in 1918.

Women that were *against* the vote being given to women have been forgotten by history and it is only fairly recently that any research has been done into this phenomenon. Again, it was mainly upper- and middle-class women that were involved in this campaign. Both the Suffragettes and the Anti-Suffrage League claimed the support of the majority of women, but it is noticeable that the Anti-

Suffrage League was able to gather 250,000 signatures on a petition against women being able to vote.[11] It is not clear, though, what percentage of those signatures were women's.

Any historian researching this period comes up against the usual brick wall when it comes to the working classes; they tend not to leave any records behind. The general consensus seems to be, however, that ordinary women were simply apathetic when it came to female suffrage; they probably thought it had nothing to do with them. And what of the womenfolk of the Scottish Protestant underclass; what stance did they take?

Obviously, any answer to that cannot be definitive but it is possible to extrapolate given the attitudes of what was later to become The People. It is worth remembering that the Orange Order is inordinately proud of opposing the 1832 Reform Bill (see Chapter 4), so it seems highly likely that they opposed all extensions of the franchise. This, of course, would include giving the vote to women. But would the women simply go along with what their menfolk believed? The situation in Ulster can give us a major clue.

There were Suffragettes in Ireland as well, whose campaign, apparently, cut across the Unionist/Nationalist divide.[12] When it came to the crunch, however, Irish politics took precedence over those of gender and Ulster Protestant women rushed to sign *Ulster's Solemn League and Covenant*; except they did not. It is often omitted from the narrative of this event that the women actually signed a *separate* document, pledging their support for the male signatories of the Covenant.[13] Women that had campaigned for female suffrage signed this separate declaration, exposing themselves to the ridicule of Nationalist Suffragettes.[14]

With middle-class Protestant women in Ulster falling in behind their menfolk, it is more than probable that the women of the Scottish Protestant underclass followed suit. To be fair, though, the lack of outrage when only well-to-do women were given the vote in 1918 betrays an apathy about female suffrage among practically all working-class women.

An argument against women of the Scottish Protestant underclass falling into line might be Mary Barbour and the other women that organised the rent strike in Glasgow in 1915.[15] Mrs. Barbour was from Govan, where Glasgow's shipyards were based, meaning it was a leading base for the Scottish Protestant underclass and, consequently, the place where Rangers finally settled. And yet, here was this woman, part of what would become The People, taking a stance against private landlords and organising peace movements.[16] So, does that mean that we have to revise our understanding of the women of the Scottish Protestant underclass? Well, actually, no.

After the War, Mary Barbour went on to represent Govan for the Labour Party on Glasgow Corporation, both as a councillor and a bailie. It is interesting to note, however, that all the work she did was concerned with households, welfare and child care.[17] These are exactly the political concerns that many in the Anti-Suffrage League saw as 'women's issues'.

> They (the women against female suffrage) claimed that women were as capable as men, if not superior in some ways, but destined to fulfil a different role in society. Their caring and maternal role rested upon their moral strength and emotional sensitivity. These qualities would be threatened by immersion into parliamentary politics but did not preclude them from other forms of public service. Domestic strengths were needed not only in the home but also in the wider fields of education and social service. Women could contribute to and find personal fulfilment through philanthropic work or in the expanding field of local government, without trespassing on the male territory of parliamentary politics.[18]

A persuasive argument for women not voting in parliamentary elections was that they did not fight in wars so should have no say in national politics, which might involve sending men off to fight.[19] This, of course, precluded women MPs and it is interesting to note that Mary Barbour never stood for national office, even though she would have had an excellent chance of being elected. It would appear that she had a set idea of what a woman's role in politics was.

This was how things worked in Ulster too in the period before the First World War. Women's participation in the UVF was limited to being nurses and fund-raising. They were also to be responsible for indoctrinating the province's youth in the ideas of Unionism and the Protestant Ascendancy.[20] Gender roles were strictly demarcated.

It is worth contrasting women in Scottish Socialism with those elsewhere. Women played a major role in the Russian Revolution, including being involved in the fighting.[21] The same was true of the Easter Rising in 1916 in Dublin.[22] There was no revolution in Scotland for women to get involved in or not but there were women, like Mary Barbour, who were involved in Socialist politics. Granted, working-class women could not vote in general elections until 1928, but after the first female Labour MP was elected in 1929, the next was not until 1937; she also happened to be Glasgow's very first woman MP.[23]

During the 1920s and 1930s, only five women were elected to Parliament in Scotland; three of these were upper-class Tories. This dearth of female MPs, however, could be attributed to political parties not putting up enough women candidates; it tells us nothing about how women were voting. What we need to look at are the results of general elections in Scotland after 1928 to see if the coming of universal suffrage made any difference.

In the 1929 election, out of seventy-four seats, only sixteen changed hands: twelve to Labour and four to Liberal.[24] That means that fifty-eight seats were held by the same party that had won them in 1924. Some of the majorities of those new Labour seats, moreover, were wafer-thin. In Berwick and Haddington, for example, Labour's majority was only 326, while in Dunbartonshire it was 1,577.[25] It did not look as if the new female electorate had made much of a difference. Women appeared to be simply voting the same way as their menfolk; just as many people had predicted back in the days of the Suffragettes!

Of course, we have no way of knowing who these voters were, what religion, if any, they were or which football team their husbands supported. All we can surmise is that the womenfolk among The People were voting in the same way as the menfolk, nothing more. Since other women appeared to be doing the same thing, then it tells us next-to-nothing about the female contingent of The People. For that, we shall have to move away from electoral politics.

It is fortunate for our study that Northern Ireland exists, being as it is a kind of petri dish where we can view The People in something close to isolation. Miranda Alison, of the University of Warwick, made a study of women involved in the Troubles, on both sides of the conflict. What she found was that women played an active part in the Provisional IRA, including as combatants. Loyalist women, on the other hand, played a more traditional role, as nurses and the like.[26]

A rather astute Loyalist explained why this was the case. According to him, 'Republicans viewed the conflict as being a revolutionary war of resistance against the state', and

> if you are buildin' a revolutionary movement then you have to be fightin' that revolution on all fronts, and one of them is on that gender front – I mean you've gotta link your revolutions, you've gotta be all embracin' and you link yourself to human rights issues and to gender issues . . . which the republicans have done. Loyalists didn't need to.[27]

Not that anyone is advocating that a woman needs a gun to be equal to a man, but it is clear that gender equality was more pronounced on the Republican side than it was on the Loyalist. Nowadays, of course, all political parties have female representatives at Stormont. That, however, is no indication of gender equality; would anyone cite Margaret Thatcher as a great supporter of women's rights? What we need to look at is how women's lives are affected in Northern Ireland.

Two of the biggest differences from the UK that critics of the Irish Republic always used to point to were the availability of contraception and abortion. Both were illegal in Ireland long after they became freely available in the UK. Actually, however, that was not strictly true. There was one part of the UK where abortion was, and still is, not freely available. That place is Northern Ireland. And it is not the supposedly-Catholic Republicans that have consistently blocked Northern Ireland from falling into line with the rest of the UK; it is the Loyalists that have insisted on this.

As for contraception, although nominally freely available in Northern Ireland, even in the 21st Century attitudes toward condoms there have been shown to be positively archaic.[28] Education about contraception appears to be well behind the times too.[29]

It would appear that women, then, just as in 1912, take second place to Unionism in Northern Ireland. It has to be stressed, though, that many Northern-Irish women might well agree with the status-quo in the Six Counties. As we shall see in the next chapter, however, not all Unionists are happy. But what about the female members of The People in Scotland; how do they feel about the situation in Northern Ireland?

Men are still the main participants in Orange Walks in Scotland, although there seem to be as many women as men following behind and lining the streets. Since this is all about 'Protestant Culture', it is reasonable to conclude that these women support the whole idea of the 'Protestant Ascendancy' in Northern Ireland, including the laws relating to abortion. That is, of course, assuming that they actually understand the issues involved. Looking at posts on social media, it is often clear that they, along with their menfolk, do *not* understand. But, then, they do not want to understand; all that matters is that the Taigs are put in their place.

10
I Can Sing A Rainbow

When it comes to politics, the only issue that The People care about is Northern Ireland remaining part of the UK. This is the case both in Scotland and in Northern Ireland itself. For the Loyalists in Northern Ireland this is going to create a massive problem in the very near future. They are going to have to choose between this fundamental issue and their religiously-inspired policies. Their core electorate is going to demand it.

As we saw in the last chapter, Northern Ireland's laws are not the same as the rest of the UK. Not only is abortion illegal, but the Democratic Unionist Party (DUP) has ensured that discrimination against LGBT people is possibly the worst in Western Europe.[1] The DUP has a long history of opposing gay rights[2] and continues to use its veto to make sure same-sex marriages remain illegal.[3]

Away back in 1981, when AIDS was still called GRIDS (Gay-Related Immune-Deficiency Syndrome) and the press was discussing the 'Gay Plague', sexually-active homosexual men were banned from giving blood for life.[4] It took thirty years for this to be abolished but, even then, gay men had to abstain from sex for a full twelve months before giving blood.[5] Quite how anyone proves or disproves this nobody is saying and it was still discrimination since a heterosexual man could just as easily be infected with HIV. It was, though, considered a step in the right direction.

As one might expect, the DUP at Stormont made sure that Northern Ireland did not comply with this change. It took another five years for Northern Ireland to fall into line and a Sinn Fein Health Minister to do it. Embarrassingly for the DUP, she had only been in the job eight days when she lifted the lifetime ban.[6]

The homophobia of the DUP, its stance on abortion and its close connection to the fundamentalist lobby group, the Caleb Foundation[7] mean that many younger Unionists are becoming disillusioned with the party.[8] These younger people still want to stay in the UK, but do not want to live in the kind of theocratic dictatorship that the DUP envisions for Northern Ireland.

The ironic thing is that if the Six Counties were part of a united Ireland, then the voters there might well have ensured that abortion and same-sex marriages remained illegal on the whole island. Although the vote in both cases was overwhelmingly in favour, the fact is that the turnout was only 60.52% for the referendum on same-sex marriage[9] and that to legalise abortion 64.1%.[10] The Caleb Foundation, if allied to conservative Catholicism, would make a powerful lobby group in a united Ireland, while many Catholic voters would be willing to vote with the DUP if it dropped its sectarianism.

This, obviously, leaves the DUP facing a dilemma. Those younger Northern-Irish Protestants we discussed earlier feel that no party represents their interests, so they do not bother to vote at all.[11] If the DUP does not abandon its adherence to the Caleb Foundation's policies, then it risks losing everything. Its aging electorate will eventually die out, meaning that, with younger Protestants abstaining, the Republicans could win. The DUP, and other Loyalist parties, are going to have to decide what their priorities are. If they wish to remain in the UK, then they will have to abandon their religiously-inspired social policies.

There might come a time when we see the LGBT Rainbow Loyal Defenders marching along the Shankill Road on the 12th of July. One wonders how the old guard in the Orange Order would feel about that! Would they be happy marching with people that are openly lesbian, gay, bisexual and transsexual? It is something that they might well have to tolerate. Presumably, as long as there are no Catholic lesbian, gay, bisexual and transsexual folk turning up, they will just grit their teeth and bear it.

It certainly shows the size of the challenge Loyalist politicians face. But, it is not just The People in Northern Ireland that those politicians need to keep sweet; there are The People in Scotland to consider as well. And those People in Scotland want Northern Ireland to remain in the UK, no matter what the cost.

A kind of symbiosis has developed between the two sets of The People on either side of the North Channel. To The People in Scotland, support for the Protestants of Northern Ireland gives a sense of purpose and meaning to their religion. After all, even they can probably see that a football team is not the best thing on which to base one's religious faith. And the idea of Protestant Ascendancy fits in neatly with their notions of their own supremacy. For their part, the upholders of the Protestant Ascendancy in Northern Ireland rely on The People in Scotland to rally to the cause if necessary.

And rally to the cause The People most certainly do. When it comes to politics, it is all they care about, even if it is to the detriment of themselves and their families. A prime example is the debate over Scotland becoming independent. None of The People even considered the economic or social implications, even though they used such rationalisations to cover up the true reason why they were vehemently opposed to an independent Scotland. That reason was to keep Northern Ireland a part of the UK.

The truth is that most English people wish that Northern Ireland would just disappear. In fact, many of them regret ever setting foot on the island. Even Tories are sick of it hanging round their necks, though they have recently relied on the DUP to stay in power. Boris Johnson's father, Stanley Johnson, who was a Conservative MEP himself, said that, rather than disrupt Britain's plans to leave the EU with arguments over hard or soft borders, 'if the Irish want to shoot each other, they will shoot each other'.[12] In other words, the Irish, North and South, could go to hell.

If the Westminster Government were ever to abandon Northern Ireland, however, The People in Scotland would be screaming for independence and would then hope to join with Northern Ireland in some type of Orangeland. As it is, Westminster is determined to hold onto Scotland, even though it is, supposedly, full of dole-scroungers that rely on England's largesse. That means, of course, that Westminster is stuck with Northern Ireland.

So, The People in Northern Ireland rely on The People in Scotland to keep them in the UK, while England relies on The People in Northern Ireland to influence The People in Scotland to keep Scotland in the UK. Meanwhile, the people in Scotland are stuck with The People in Scotland, voting and campaigning on behalf of Northern Ireland. It all gets a bit confusing.

In November 2018 a proverbial toe was dipped into the proverbial water. The new club at Ibrox, which I have christened 'Neo-Gers', made an announcement that looked like an attempt to drag The People, kicking and screaming, into the 21st Century. It was a new supporters' group, called Ibrox Pride, for Neo-Gers fans that happened to be members of the LGBT community.[13] If this went down okay with The People, then it might well lead to a new direction for the DUP. Unfortunately, The People responded exactly as you might expect.

> Vile.[14]

> Give them their own wee section in the stadium, they can brighten it with some throws over the seats and a nice pair of curtains at the entrance from the concourse to the passageway.[15]

> I mind a game at Airdrie, Rangers fans chanting 'he's gay he's bent his arse is up for rent Fashanu Fashanu' Airdrie fans responded with 'he's black he's gay he plays for Airdire Fashanu'
> They were the days, none of this pandering PC shite.[16]

> So long as they've separate toilets and changing rooms from straight ppl[17]

> 4 poofs has (sic) a dream.[18]

> Coplandbear will be relieved to hear that this puts an end to the safe standing debate. Nae cunt wants a gayer staring at yer arse for over 90 minutes.[19]

> Encouraging Sodomites is against Christian teachings, I'm horrified and will be informing the club of my disgust.[20]

It looked as if this harmless gesture had not gone down too well with The People. With those kinds of attitudes, it hardly seemed likely that the DUP would be making changes to the way they treated the LGBT community. Besides, the DUP had bigger fish to fry.

The referendum about whether to leave the EU or not in 2016 resulted in Northern Ireland, like Scotland, voting to remain. The votes of the UK as a whole, however, were overwhelmed by those of the English, especially those of the denizens of the densely-populated south of England. There the majority voted to leave the EU, which meant that Scotland and Northern Ireland would be dragged out too.

The DUP had campaigned for the 'Leave' side so were overjoyed at the result. It was one of those occasions when the party decided that Northern Ireland was an integral part of the United Kingdom. This is not always the case as we have already seen. When it comes to things like same-sex marriage and abortion, the DUP always wants to take a divergent path from that of Westminster. There are no claims then that Northern Ireland is as much a part of the UK as England and Wales.

The Ulster Unionist Party (UUP), which used to be the leading Unionist party, had campaigned for a 'Remain' vote but changed their minds after the result. Rather pettily, the reason for this was to stand with the DUP against Sinn Fein.[21] With the SDLP keen on keeping Northern Ireland in the EU, the issue was being made into a Unionist vs. Nationalist one.

To say that nobody completely understood what Brexit was all about would be an understatement. Even those voting were confused. While those wanting to remain in the EU argued about financial figures on the side of a bus, the 'Leave' campaign mostly concentrated on immigration. It was no secret that racism played a huge part in people voting to leave.[22] Stupidity was also a factor.

After the Brexit vote, not only Europeans resident in England were targeted by racists but Muslims and anyone else that those racists considered non-British. They believed that the 'Leave' victory meant that all 'foreigners' now had to leave Britain.[23] In fact, figures showed that hate crimes in England and Wales rose by 41% in the month after the referendum.[24] Surprisingly, there was a decline in such crimes in Northern Ireland. Superintendent Paula Hilman of the PSNI, however, expressed the opinion that hate crimes were going unreported.[25]

Another factor in people voting 'Leave' was anti-intellectualism.[26] This is generally the way with right-wing organisations: Nazi Germany, for example, removed academic studies from schools,[27] and held mass burnings of intellectual books.[28] Anti-intellectualism was also a feature of McCarthyism in America, with most hatred directed toward the intelligentsia that had worked for Roosevelt in framing the *New Deal*. It has become remarkably easy to use anti-intellectualism for political ends in the USA,[29] as the election of Donald Trump to the position of president shows.[30]

Like the infamous Joseph McCarthy, Trump and his supporters frame their anti-intellectualism in terms of being *anti-elite*.[31] Such arguments against the 'elite' are familiar in the UK as well; Nigel Farage used the same rabble-rousing tactics during the Brexit referendum.[32] In fact, such rhetoric has even been employed by that one-time member of the truly elitist Bullingdon Club, Boris Johnson![33]

As we saw in Chapter 8, despite desperate arguments to the contrary, anti-intellectualism has long been a feature among those Ulster Protestants that identify themselves as the 'PUL Community'. Even if their own leaders expressed anything clever or common-sense, they simply did not want to know. In 1921, for example, Edward Carson, that great symbol of Protestant Unionism, said the following,

> We used to say that we could not trust an Irish parliament in Dublin to do justice to the Protestant minority. Let us take care that that reproach can no longer be made against your parliament, and from the outset let them see that the Catholic minority have nothing to fear from a Protestant majority.[34]

History shows that Carson's words were completely ignored. Partisan pseudo-historian Ruth Dudley Edwards quotes a David Trimble speech about Scots and Ulster Protestants contributing to the Enlightenment. She then continues:

> It's all part of an old battle between Enlightenment values and Romanticism. Adherence to Roman Catholicism required absolute obedience: in reaction, Scots and Ulster-Scots Presbyterians were leading figures in intellectual enquiry.[35]

That, however, is utter nonsense. Perhaps the greatest philosopher to come from the British Isles was David Hume. Despite Hume's reputation among academics in England and abroad, he was refused a chair at both Glasgow and Edinburgh Universities simply because he was an atheist. After his death, it was French philosophers that kept his reputation alive, while he was largely forgotten in his native Scotland until the 20th Century.

The contention that Protestantism was somehow responsible for the Scottish Enlightenment is a rather ridiculous one. Scotland was not the only country to contribute to the Enlightenment and not all the great thinkers of the period came from a Protestant background. In fact, there was more than a hint of anti-religiousness among the thinkers of the Enlightenment, although those in Scotland probably did their best to hide it; Scottish universities were firmly under the sway of the Church of Scotland, after all. One might as well credit Catholicism for Voltaire.

If Protestantism, or, rather, Presbyterianism, especially of the Scottish and Ulster varieties, had one major feature it was that its adherents *knew* that they were right. The truth was in the Bible; there was no need to go seeking it elsewhere. This was the state of mind expressed by Ian Paisley and inherited by the DUP. And, of course, anti-intellectualism was part-and-parcel of this belief.[36]

Remember those generations of knuckle-draggers being produced by the Church of Scotland that we spoke about in Chapter 2? They reached their apotheosis in The People, both in Ulster and in Scotland. Education was for mugs; God would provide for His People. In fact, society at large encouraged this attitude; but more about that later.

So, now we are stuck with these barely-evolved creatures, who, unfortunately, are allowed to vote as if they were proper human beings. As mentioned earlier, these violent brutes have been led to believe that an independent Scotland would put the future of Northern Ireland being part of the UK at risk. They have also been indoctrinated with the insane belief that everyone is out to destroy their club. These two issues have combined to convince them that Protestantism is under threat throughout the British Isles and it is up to them to defend it.

For decades The People in Scotland believed that the Labour Party was run by, and for the benefit of, Catholics. We are all familiar with the mad rantings of the character that calls himself PZJ, who has wasted most of his adult years in trying to prove that Celtic FC benefited financially from a close relationship by the Labour-run

Glasgow Council. DUP members raised his concerns in the EU and instigated an investigation that found no foundation at all for PZJ's ramblings. Apparently, he is still pursuing his fantasies but, at present, his Twitter account has been suspended for the umpteenth time.

The political landscape has changed in Scotland, but The People still view things in the same terms. With Labour now almost an irrelevance in Scottish politics, The People have transferred their ire to the SNP. It seems that the SNP is trying to eliminate 'Protestantism', wants to hand Northern Ireland over to the Irish Republic and establish a Catholic republic in Scotland. The only friends The People have are in the Conservative Party, which has once more taken to calling itself the Conservative and *Unionist* Party in Scotland.

In Chapter 4 it was mentioned, in passing, that there were those that saw Rangers as simply being their football team. To such folk, that was where it ended. Unlike The People, they were not going to let their team dictate their politics. Such individuals still exist, although they are certainly in a minority among the Ibrox horde.

Since Catholics only make up around 15% of the Scottish population,[37] it makes no sense to claim that it is they that put the SNP in charge at Holyrood. And the 27% of the Glasgow population that claimed to be Catholic in the 2011 Census[38] would hardly have been able to elect an SNP council on its own. It stands to reason that there must be SNP voters among the Ibrox support. To The People, such folk are nothing short of traitors.

> I'd have political affiliations linked to whether you could buy a ST or a ticket or not.
> Fucking Scottish Natzi Party wankers would be instantly excluded, no appeal allowed. Followed by a swift execution.[39]

> They're not real Rangers fans.
> It's quite simple to be honest.[40]

> When you see the taigish antics and ramblings of the Yes movement I find it utterly astonishing that anyone who follows our club could relate to that pish.[41]

> The SNP have metamorphosised politically into the very antithesis of anything Unionist and Protestant, and anything that represents Unionism and Protestantism is in their sights.
>
> Sturgeon has been bypassed, Salmond is gone, this party has been corrupted from the inside and is now a puppet being worked from underneath by anti-British Republican Roman Catholics who take their lead, their culture, their prejudices and their vices from Sinn Fein in Ireland.[42]

There was no doubting, then, what the political leanings of The People were. Just in case there was any doubt, one of their number posted the following on Twitter: 'If you are a protestant vote Tory it's for QUEEN and COUNTRY.'[43]

Of course, with the DUP on the side of leaving the EU, The People just had to follow follow on. And when the Tories were reliant on the DUP in order to form a government, The People must have felt that all their Christmases had come at once. Theresa May's government handed the DUP £1billion to ensure their support and was working apace to get the UK out of the EU. Things could not have been better; until, that is, the bombshell arrived.

Right from the start, the DUP was against the Good Friday Agreement, campaigning for the deal not to be ratified in the referendum.[44] Ever since, DUP politicians have done their best to ensure that power sharing at Stormont has not run smoothly. In fact, DUP leader, Arlene Foster was quoted as saying that the Good Friday Agreement was not 'sacrosanct'.[45] It certainly should not interfere with Brexit. Unfortunately, Theresa May did not quite feel the same way.

Amid all the jargon of the proposed Brexit agreement one thing stood out for the DUP: that the maintaining of a 'soft border' between Northern Ireland and the Irish Republic would mean customs checks on goods crossing from NI to Britain.[46] This would, in effect, almost divorce NI from the UK and bring it closer to the Irish Republic. Despite the economic benefits of such an arrangement, the whole thing was anathema to the DUP. It also angered The People.

> Let it be known to Mrs may that any move to remove Northern Ireland from the union in anyway shall be met with resistance. Violent or otherwise. We shall not be the generation to fail Ulster. Feriens Tego.[47]

Well, it seemed as if Theresa May's Brexit plans acted like a stick poked into The People's nest. As usual, they were convinced that the whole thing was a big conspiracy against them. If they were to turn their backs on the Tories, who would they have left?

Fortunately for The People, and rather unfortunately for the rest of us, it looks as if the world is going back in time to meet them. Fascist groups have proliferated throughout Europe in the past few years, while the rise of Donald Trump in America has given a fillip to the far right all over the world. Francoists have come crawling out of the woodwork in Spain, while Jair Bolsonaro, an extreme far-right and militarist candidate, won the presidency in Brazil. Fascist salutes have become a common sight everywhere. Maybe the future belongs to The People. It is a frightening thought.

11
Your Own Personal Jesus

Everybody knows what happened in 2012, although different folk put their own spin on it. Essentially, Rangers, that great church of The People died. No sooner was this announced, though, than it came back from the dead, so to speak. Now, The People did not need to rely any more on the saviour of any other religion; they now had their own. Unfortunately, Jesus was not the only one to die and then come back in the Bible.

The Beast in the Book of Revelation came out of the sea with 'We Are The People' marked on its forehead and five false stars on its breast. Okay, I made that up, but The Beast certainly died and was resurrected. A second Beast, also called the False Prophet, appeared to get everyone to worship the first Beast that had come back from the dead. Dave King, anyone?

The People even have their very own 'Mark of the Beast', without which nobody can expect to do business, shop or even walk down the street in safety. Rather than have it tattooed on their hands or foreheads, The People wear the mark. Actually, some of them do have it tattooed about their persons and worship it almost as much as they do their club, their redeemer. It is only worn once a year by most folk, but The People desperately want it to be a permanent feature. The article in question is, of course, the poppy.

I remember when I was a child back in the 1960s and early 1970s, you would put money in a tin and put your poppy aside for Remembrance Sunday. Some folk would wear their poppy in the week leading up to Remembrance Sunday but, for the most part, it was kept safe so that it would look pristine on the day. Gradually, this has changed and, nowadays, not only do folk wear them all throughout November but in October as well. And this is no longer a choice; it is an obligation.

And, not only has the period when one wears the poppy changed; the whole meaning behind it has changed too. Back in the day, it was mostly about WWI and the sheer waste of life that conflict entailed. Everybody understood that, although WWII could be morally justified and portrayed as a war of 'Good versus Evil', the First World war most definitely could not. It achieved nothing and the changes it wrought were not worth celebrating. Essentially, the Great War was viewed as the epitome of a waste of young men's lives and Remembrance Sunday was a kind of promise that it would not be allowed to happen again.

Those days seem like centuries ago and, rather than making sure that a conflict such as WWI never happens again, the poppy has become the symbol of the warmonger. Not only that, but everything about WWI has been twisted to make it appear as if it was a war for freedom and democracy. Instead of regretting the throwing away of the lives of all those young men, we are now supposed to celebrate it, as if it were something wonderful. Even the famous war poets are used and abused to fit this new agenda.

People of my age will remember studying war poets, like Wilfred Owen and Siegfried Sassoon, at school. I do not know what happens at school these days but, in the media, Owen and Sassoon have been pretty much replaced with Rupert Brooke and Laurence Binyon, neither of whom saw any fighting and whose most famous works were written in the early years of the War. Even Owen's most well-known poem, *Dulce et Decorum est*, has its main, and most powerful, lines quoted completely out of context. Quite often, these days, those final lines,

> The old Lie: *Dulce et decorum est*
> *Pro patria mori*.[1]

are quoted without the first three words, turning it into an old-fashioned glorification of war.

Of course, with their long-standing proclivity for worshipping Mars, The People have been all over this new style of Remembrance Sunday. We saw in Chapter 7 the extreme measures that The People go to in order to 'celebrate' Remembrance Day, but there is far more to it than that. The poppy has, rather ironically, become the symbol of British nationalism and all that it entails.

Every tuppeny-ha'penny would-be Fuhrer, from arch-Brexiteer Nigel Farage to Muslim-baiter Stephen Christopher Yaxley-Lennon *aka* Tommy Robinson, uses the poppy to galvanise his supporters. It has become the emblem of the racist, the bootboy, the Telegraph-reading old colonel that misses the Empire, the xenophobe, the homophobe and the psychotic nutter that desperately wants to kill somebody.[2] Above all, though, it is the badge of the dark side of Britishness; hence the allegiance of The People.

To The People themselves, though, this is far from the truth. In their view, they are the good guys and everybody else is bad to them. It is the rest of the world that are following the Antichrist and they, as God's Chosen People, that are suffering for their faith. Like all good Protestants from centuries ago, they hope and pray for the *End of Days* to come; especially before Celtic win ten league titles in a row.

Almost as soon as the Reformation started, the yearning for the *End of Days* was palpable; and it was to continue thereafter. It was every Protestant's duty, not just to hope for and expect the *End of Days*, but to work towards bringing it about. That was why Oliver Cromwell brought the Jews back to England; the Book of Revelation predicts that the Jews would convert to Christianity in the last days.

In more modern times, fundamentalist and evangelical Christians were to the forefront in founding the state of Israel and continue to support it, no matter what it does. Jesus is going to come back to Jerusalem and the Jews need to be there, in charge, before this can come about.[3] A serious fly in the ointment is the fact that there is a mosque on Temple Mount in Jerusalem, from where the prophet Mohammed is believed to have ascended to Heaven. This possibly explains the hostility of American evangelicals toward Muslims.[4]

The People, however, do not have much truck with messianic predictions about Jerusalem; they have their own temple, after all. They also have their own version of Mecca; the Holy State of Northern Ireland. Muslims are expected to make a sacred pilgrimage, the *hajj*, at least once during their lifetime. This is to be carried out during the month of *Dhu al-Hijja*. The People are under the same kind of obligation and have to visit Northern Ireland, at least once in their lifetime, during the month of July.

We have all seen pictures of pilgrims at Mecca, walking around the *Kabaa* while praying. The People do the same sort of thing, visiting all the sacred sites while singing and chanting holy verses. Northern Ireland, however, is much more of a sacred place than Mecca could ever be. It is The People's equivalent of Medina as well since it is the birthplace of the Orange Order, which permeates just about every aspect of The People's religion.

Like Protestants of old, and like fundamentalist and evangelical Christians everywhere, The People also look forward to the *End of Days*. While more powerful concerns rely on fracking and armies to start the prophesied earthquakes, wars and rumours of wars, the efforts of The People appear rather puny. They try their best, though, jumping up and down in unison, singing *Bouncy Bouncy* and trashing every town and city they visit. In many respects, however, The People's view is that we are already in the middle of the events of Revelation.

If you read the Book of Revelation, you will discover that Christ is not going to make His Second Coming a quiet affair. He is going to come in glory to conquer evil, with the help of the righteous. He is then going to reign for a thousand years, the Millennium; a time when all the good people in the world are going to be happy.[5]

In case you are unaware, *Christ* was not Jesus's surname; He and his earthly family were not introduced to people as Mr and Mrs Christ and their son, Jesus Christ. The word *Christ* comes from the Greek word *Christos* (Χριστος), which has the same meaning as the Hebrew word, *Messiah*. It refers to the *Saviour*, the *Redeemer*, in both Judaism and Christianity. It does not specifically say that *Jesus* will come back in the Book of Revelation so, this time, it might not be a bloke with long hair and a beard. Who is to say what form *Christ* will take in the Second Coming? It might be more than one person, or even an abstract concept; a football team, perhaps.

This is the way The People read the Book of Revelation; the Messiah, their team, has already arrived and they look forward to the Millennium. During that period, The People's team, which they still insist on calling 'Rangers', is going to win a thousand league titles in a row, as well as the Scottish Cup and the League Cup in each of those thousand years. First, though, there is the little matter of Armageddon.

According to the Book of Revelation, there is going to be a huge battle pitting Christ and the Righteous against all the nations of the world, led by the Beast and the False Prophet. The People believe this is already happening and that all the world's forces are ranged against them and their team. They know, however, that this is going to change and that there will be a great wailing and gnashing of teeth, especially among Celtic supporters.

Of course, a team cannot lead The People into battle against their many enemies, but, again, according to the Book of Revelation, help is going to come in a familiar form.

> And I saw heaven opened, and behold a white horse; and he that sat upon him was called Faithful and True, and in righteousness he doth judge and make war.[6]

So, it seems that King Billy, on his famous white charger, is going to come down from Heaven and lead The People to victory. Until that glorious day, however, The People need a more down-to-earth warrior on their side.

Away back in the days of the Crusades, a rumour circulated throughout Europe that there was a rich, powerful, Christian kingdom, ruled by a man of faith called Prester John.[7] All that was needed was to find this individual and he, and his mighty army, would drive back the Muslim hordes from Eastern Europe and the Holy Land. Prester John's kingdom was variously thought to be in India, the Middle East, Cathay and Africa. Every time explorers were disappointed to discover that Prester John's kingdom was not where they thought it was, the fabled land's location moved to somewhere else.

The People have their own version of Prester John, although he does not have a name. Like many in medieval Europe, they believe he resides in fair Cathay, which medieval explorers were shocked and surprised to discover was simply China.[8] Many are the times it has been reported in the media that a major investor from Hong Kong or the Chinese mainland is interested in putting major funds into the Ibrox club. These stories are more in hope than expectation and show the desperation of The People to find somebody, anybody, to aid them in their quest for world domination.

In the meantime, The People make sure that their religion remains unsullied and their holy temple not profaned by the agents of evil. This normally takes the form of banning any expression of Catholicism, especially the making of the sign of the cross. Such a fuss is made over players blessing themselves that Celtic goalkeeper, Artur Boruc, ended up being cautioned by the police for doing it within the holy grounds of Ibrox.[9] Catholics that play for the Ibrox team, meanwhile, are warned not to make this offensive gesture, especially at their home ground.[10]

Away back in the good, old days, it was an unwritten rule that Catholics were not allowed into Rangers in any capacity. Apparently, though, some managed to slip under the radar; but, as long as they kept their heads down, then nobody was any the wiser. Nowadays, Catholics openly sign for Neo-Gers and nobody says a word; unless, of course, they are not up to scratch. If that happens, then they are 'Fenian bastards', who should not be at the club.

In the main, however, The People tend to turn a blind eye to Catholic players at their sacred club, possibly comforting themselves with the story of the *Curse of Ham*. This charming tale used to be used to justify the enslavement of African people, so it would not be a surprise if The People employ it in a similar manner.

> And Ham, the father of Canaan, saw the nakedness of his father, and told his two brethren without. And Shem and Japheth took a garment, and laid it upon both their shoulders, and went backward, and covered the nakedness of their father; and their faces were backward, and they saw not their father's nakedness. And Noah awoke from his wine, and knew what his younger son had done unto him. And he said, Cursed be Canaan; a servant of servants shall he be unto his brethren.[11]

For many players filthy lucre overcomes any scruples they might have about their religious beliefs. A case in point is Spaniard Nacho Novo. This character was never a great footballer but has acquired the epithet 'legend' by belly-crawling to the lowest common denominator among The People.

Martin O'Neill called Novo a 'decent squad player' and that is exactly the way he was used at Rangers. He rarely started a match, being used mainly as a substitute. Although Celtic did express an interest in him when he was at Dundee, that interest was quickly dropped; he was not worth the money being asked for him.[12] And yet, he had the cheek to call his autobiography *I Said No thanks*.[13]

But Novo went further than just lying about turning Celtic down to endear himself to The People; much further. He likes to attend the 12th of July parades in Belfast and is even present at the *bonefires* on the night before,[14] where images and effigies of his fellow Catholics are burned to a soundtrack of bigoted songs of hate. There are even stories about him posing for pictures with Loyalist terrorists and singing anti-Catholic songs. It is these actions, rather than his football prowess, that has made him a 'legend' among The People. A *soup-taker* like Novo is the ideal kind of Catholic to play at Ibrox.

The weird thing about The People's religion is that John Calvin and John Knox would probably recognise it as Protestantism more than they would modern Protestant churches. In a statement of its beliefs, the Free Church of Scotland says that, 'The gospel message is for everyone.'[15] Knox would have had a fit if he had read that! Then again, it could be argued that although the 'gospel message' is for everyone, *salvation* is most definitely not.

This blog, by a Free Church minister, however, makes plain that, nowadays, salvation is for everybody.[16] Not only would Calvin and Knox take issue with that, they would also be infuriated by the idea, implicit in the text of the blog, that one should *hate the sin, not the sinner*. Calvinism was all about hating the sinner as well and, most certainly, those identifying as homosexual would find themselves facing excommunication, if not the business end of a rope.

The modern Church of Scotland, meanwhile, would drive Knox apoplectic. Its General Assembly decided years ago to allow gay clergy[17] and has even been discussing the possibility of allowing same-sex marriages.[18] The Protestant churches in Scotland have come a long way.

The early Calvinists would readily recognise the elitism and sense of entitlement of The People as Protestantism. In fact, the only thing they would find distinctly *un*Protestant about The People is their love of ceremony and symbolism. As we saw in Chapter 7, this has become an essential part of The People's religion and has become even more important since the death and resurrection of their club.

At every home game, and sometimes even when they are playing away, The People like to re-enact Jesus's triumphant entry into Jerusalem. As the Gospels relate, the people of Jerusalem threw palm fronds in front of Jesus as He rode in on a donkey. Palm fronds are pretty light and would not make it onto the pitch if The People threw them, so they improvise. They throw coins, lighters and batteries onto the pitch to greet their team. It is considered lucky to be hit by one of these palm-frond substitutes.

The People see themselves as the only *real* Protestants left; even the hellfire-and-brimstone preachers of Northern Ireland do not come close. Some of these characters turn up to shout through a microphone at people on Glasgow Green at the end of the big July parade. Quite often they find themselves having empty beer cans bounced off their forehead because they are disturbing a group of The People that are listening to some Orange songs on a CD player.

And since The People see themselves as the only Protestants, they automatically claim that any attack against them is an attack on *Protestantism*. Rather bizarrely, the media and the authorities do nothing to disabuse The People of this delusion.

In July 2018, a priest was attacked outside his church while an Orange Walk was passing. Some of his parishioners were attacked as well.[19] It seemed that it was not one of the 'official marchers' that carried out the deed but one of the usual hangers-on that walk behind them. Strangely, though, nobody saw a thing, despite all the police and Orange Order stewards in attendance. One cannot help but wonder if they *chose* not to see anything.

Unbelievably, another Orange Walk was due to take place past the church just a couple of weeks after this incident. There were two weddings due to take place that day, which left the priest worrying about what might happen.[20] The Orange Lodges involved decided to postpone this march, apparently in agreement with Glasgow Council.[21] When the Council asked Lodges to re-route a planned Walk at the end of August, however, the Lodges took the huff and cancelled the whole march.[22] A spokesman for the Orange Order in Scotland said,

> The decision to withdraw the application was made by members of the local Lodge. There is considerable alarm amongst members now that Glasgow City Council has in-effect declared some streets as no-go zones based on religion.[23]

As far as most folk are aware, the Orange Order is *not* a religion. As middle-class Protestants, and Protestant churches, deserted the Order in droves, it has percolated down to simply being the preserve of The People. And, since they see themselves as the last bastion of Protestantism, then it is easy for them to argue that banning an Orange Walk from going past a Catholic church is proof of an anti-Protestant agenda.

They claim that Orange Walks are just to celebrate their Protestant 'culture' and to uphold the Protestant faith. Surely the best way to do that would be to go to church services of a Sunday, rather than staggering along Scotland's streets, drunk on cheap cider and Buckfast, telling folk that they should 'go home'. The truth is, however, that they are just a shower of bigots, which is why they insist on marching past Catholic churches. What is the point of displays of bigotry if they cannot be guaranteed to meet folk that they can be bigoted against?

A small group assembled outside Glasgow City Chambers on Saturday 24th November 2018 to protest at Glasgow Council's 'anti-Protestantism'. One of their number read out a prepared speech, in which he said,

> Councillor Aitken has gone as far as to write articles vilifying our culture, heritage and religious beliefs and tar every member of the Protestant community in Glasgow with the same brush that we are bigots and hooligans simply because we wish to express our culture in the same manner as others do.[24]

What 'others' did they mean? Nobody else holds so-called religious marches during which they halt outside churches to let the congregation know how much they hate them and telling them to 'go home'. As for 'every member of the Protestant community', not every Protestant feels the need to express hatred for others and are quite content to attend their own church services and let other folk attend theirs. The People are the only group that behaves in this way. But, then, since they see themselves as the only, true Protestants, they feel justified in calling GCC 'anti-Protestant'. The speech continued by saying,

> It begs the question – is there an SNP-driven agenda against the Protestant communities of Glasgow?[25]

We already know why The People hate the SNP; the thought that an independent Scotland might lead to Northern Ireland leaving the UK frightens the life out of them. It is understandable, perhaps, that they might imagine that Glasgow Council, run by the SNP since 2017, has it in for them; their paranoia would demand no less. But they were paranoid about GCC long before the SNP took over.

As mentioned in Chapter 10, a character calling himself PZJ and somebody running a blog called *footballtaxhavens* both contended that Celtic had benefited from spurious land deals with Glasgow Council.[26] They even managed to rope the European Commission into things and were disappointed when it was concluded that neither Celtic nor GCC had anything worth investigating.

The thing is, Glasgow Council, in the days of those supposedly-dodgy land deals, was run by the Labour Party. Apparently, Labour was full of the same Celtic-loving, terrorist-supporting, Protestant-hating types that comprised the SNP. It looked as if there was nobody The People could trust. Maybe the only answer was for the DUP to stand in the next council elections!

Things get even crazier than that. In 2015, Neo-Gers, the new Ibrox club, banned Robocop lookalike Chris McLaughlin for having the nerve to report that some of The People had been arrested for sectarian behaviour. BBC Scotland responded by boycotting Ibrox completely; no cameras, no radio commentary and relying on news agencies for reports.[27] The attitude of The People toward BBC Scotland was nothing if not predictable.

> BBC Pacific Quay is infested, utterly infested. Due to a recruitment policy initiated by an Opus DEI senior director.... who went on to join the SNP wouldn't you know.[28]

> I am delighted that the unionist and Rangers boycotting of that rancid cesspit of anti protestant (sic) sectarian bigotry is having an impact.[29]

Such is the mad, religious fervour of The People. They are absolutely convinced that the whole of Scotland, the UK, in fact, the world, is in thrall to the Vatican and harbours a deep hatred of Protestants; i.e. The People. They see conspiracy everywhere and exaggerate every incident that goes against them, while ignoring completely those that go their way.

A case in point is the aftermath of referee Willie Collum showing Daniel Candeias a second yellow card and sending him off in a Neo-Gers match against St. Mirren. The Ibrox club complained bitterly, even going to the extent of saying,

> This is by no means the first time errors of judgment have been made in matches involving this official and clearly there is an underlying issue which requires to be addressed.[30]

Understandably, the SFA charged the club with bringing the game into disrepute, along with other charges.[31] As usual, though, the Ibrox club is convinced, along with The People, that it is completely in the right. Other clubs have faced similar charges for accusing referees of bias, but Neo-Gers and its support consider themselves to be above the law. In fact, The People have convinced themselves that sinister (i.e. Papist) forces are at work everywhere.[32]

Many religions have certain things that they regard as anathema; Jews will not touch pork or shellfish, Muslims, similarly, find pork offensive and Christian groups, like the Jehovah's Witnesses and the Mormons, will not eat black pudding or anything made from blood. The People are no different in this respect. It is not any kind of food that they find anathema, however; it is a colour.

Remember, when you were wee, how you would always go for the green one if you were offered a sweet? You would even fight to get your hands on the lime-flavoured *Opal Fruit* if an open bag was held in front of you and others. It was as if choosing a different colour would be a betrayal of your team. Even if you preferred the taste of the strawberry one, you would still go for the green one out of a childish, misguided sense of loyalty.

When I was a teacher, I used to get small children showing their love of Rangers, and hatred of Celtic, by refusing to touch anything green. This would result in paintings of blue trees and a complete lack of grass; only the sky was done in the right colour. They would not touch green pencils, green counting cubes or even books with green covers. It could be annoying but quite comical.

While most of us grow out of this nonsense, The People carry it on into adulthood. There are grown men and women out there that have never tasted limeade, guacamole or mint-choc-chip ice-cream because they will not touch anything green! When you get to that age, however, it is no longer a cute and comical misguided loyalty to your team; it is nothing short of insanity.

I remember reading one character that, for years, refused to use the old Glasgow Corporation buses because, at one time, they used to be painted green and white. It must have been quite a relief for his poor feet when the colour of the buses changed to orange! It would not be so bad if that was just one individual but there are plenty of others that display similarly ludicrous behaviour.

Sports writer Hugh Keevins had the following tale to tell about ex-Rangers player John 'Bomber' Brown:

> We were at the St Andrews Sporting Club for a night of wine-and-dine boxing and dinner had reached the dessert course.
> That's normally the point in the evening by which the red wine has kicked in and conviviality is at its height, but the menu got in the way on this occasion.
> The jelly served up turned out to be lime in flavour and the ice cream was of the vanilla variety.
> The colour co-ordination was indigestible for Bomber and he pushed his plate to one side with the kind of authority he used to exert over opposing attackers when he was wearing a Rangers jersey.[33]

Ex-Rangers player Mel Sterland also told the story about how he once turned up at training wearing a green tie. He was gently told off about it by Ally McCoist, they all had a good laugh and 'there was no issue at all'. So, no heavy-handed warnings, apparently, but it is clear that Sterland never wore that colour of apparel again.[34]

There have been rumours for years that food outlets at Ibrox are not allowed to sell limeade, Peperami or anything green or in a green packet. Nobody has ever denied this, and it certainly would fit in with all the other stuff we know about how they view the colour green at Ibrox. If the club behaves in this childish manner, then how can anybody expect different from The People?

But, then, are Celtic supporters not just as bad, assiduously avoiding the colours blue and orange? Well, not quite. Back in February 2017, many of The People were outraged at their team's players sporting green football boots.[35] As usual, the Daily Record tried to drag Celtic supporters into things. There were Celtic players wearing blue boots but, unfortunately for the Record's agenda, nobody among the Celtic support felt the need to complain. Nobody cared.

Of course, it was only a few months later that Mad Pedro banned green boots at Ibrox altogether.[36] This ban might have disappeared along with Pedro, but The People were adamant that it should remain. They were driven to anger, yet again, at the sight of new signing, Lassana Coulibaly, turning up to training in July 2018 wearing green boots.[37] After the complaints of The People on social media, that particular colour of boots was not seen on Coulibaly's feet again.

Meanwhile, at Celtic Park, any colour of boot was acceptable; it was the feet inside that counted. Players were seen frequently in blue boots, while Scott Brown occasionally wore orange ones. Nobody, however, gave a damn and there was no question of bans being imposed.

But The People's hatred of the colour green is not just confined to their team's boots. In July 2017, many of them made the trip down to Yorkshire to watch their team take on Sheffield Wednesday in a friendly. While they were there, some of them decided to attack a pensioner that is well known for collecting money for Macmillan Cancer Support. The man was subjected to verbal abuse, roughed up and his comedy wig and other items stolen. His crime was that he was dressed in green, the colour of the Macmillan charity.[38] The poor man was fortunate not to be badly hurt.

What The People find anathema, though, extends beyond the colour green. Anything to do with Celtic, Catholicism or Ireland, even anything that they *think* has to do with Celtic, Catholicism or Ireland, is immediately hateful to them. This can often be quite ridiculous.

Celtic began doing 'The Huddle' in 1995 and certainly was not the first sports team, or even football team to do it.[39] To The People, though, whoever did it first is completely beside the point; Celtic do it, so that is reason enough to hate it. That was why they were over the moon when one of their players, Andy Halliday, performed a rather pathetic little ritual of his own.

Halliday was on loan at Azerbaijan club, Gabala, and, before a Europa League qualifying match, the team gathered together in a 'huddle'. Halliday, however, refused to take part and stood instead with his hands clasped behind his back.[40] He was part of the huddle but, the again, manifestly not.

The way The People responded to this, you would have thought that Halliday had scored the winning goal for Neo-Gers in the Champions League final.[41] No doubt he will be referred to in the near future as a 'legend'. The People are certainly easily pleased. One of them, in reply to another, also let slip the overriding principle of The People's hatred.

> They (Celtic) didn't invent huddles ffs
>
> But they do it so fuck up[42]

But, back to The People's new soteriology. Something that has almost puzzled me about Calvinism is why Christ had to come to Earth at all since it has already been decided who is going to be saved and who is going to be damned to Hell for all eternity. What was the point? The only possible explanation is that Christ died and was resurrected for the rest of us, not the Elect. He was wasting His time, though, since we are all destined for the Big Bad Fire.

Maybe, in some way, the Elect were contaminated by the rest of us and *that* is why Christ had to die on the cross. After all, God's Chosen People were incapable of sin, were they not? So, that will be it; all we miserable sinners tainted the Elect, so Christ had to come down to do a clean-up job.

It stands to reason that The People's new soteriology will work in the same way. So, the next time you are laughing at The People and their new team, just remember – Rangers died for your sins!

12
If You're Irish Come Into The Parlour

In 1923 the General Assembly of the Church of Scotland was presented with a report called, *On the Menace of the Irish Race to our Scottish Nationality*.[1] This, frankly, racist document informed Church of Scotland policy for at least the next decade and influenced Scottish society for much longer. It blamed the Catholic Irish for all the ills in Scottish society and demanded that they all be repatriated.

This report was pretty much of its time. This was a period when racial and eugenicist theories were respectable. Even Socialist groups, like the Fabians, believed in eugenics, sometimes arguing that 'weaker' members of society should be forcibly sterilised. Part-and-parcel of all this nonsense was the idea that there were superior and inferior races. At the top of the tree were the Germanic races, which, of course, included Anglo-Saxons. Since most Scottish Protestants identified themselves as 'British', they no doubt saw themselves as being honorary Anglo-Saxons.

Certainly, Scottish Protestants looked askance at the Irish and felt justified in divorcing themselves from their Celtic and Gaelic past. The Irish were obviously inferior; did they not live in slums, work at menial jobs and never wash? Of course, no mention was made of the fact that most jobs were closed to Irish Catholics, slums were the only homes they could afford, and those slums had no running water.

The Irish Protestants that lived in Scotland mostly came from Ulster, so were originally of Scottish stock. They, of course, were not included in the Church of Scotland's diatribe. Neither were the home-grown Catholics, who, on the whole, had kept their heads down and did not cause any trouble. It was the Irish Catholics that were the problem. Memories of the navvies were still raw and had coloured the way that Irish Catholics were viewed ever since.

It was not until 2002 that the Church of Scotland apologised for its 1920s policy, while a group of bigots demonstrated outside the

Assembly, claiming that the Catholic Church was responsible for sectarian bigotry in Scotland.[2] During those eighty years the bigotry of The People was accepted by the Scottish authorities and the Scottish media.

Everyone is familiar with the sketch on *Scotch and Wry* about Rangers inadvertently signing a Catholic.[3] Hilarious as this comedy skit might seem, there is a rather sinister side to it. It was poking fun at Rangers' signing policy, but it also showed that it was an accepted part of Scottish society. Nobody was challenging this disgusting policy and it looked as if nobody wanted to. We could all have a laugh and then forget about it. If anyone did say anything serious about it, they were either ignored or shouted down. It was the Scottish way.

A rather telling part of the video is the name given to the Catholic player: Brendan O'Malley. The new Rangers player was not just a Catholic; he was an *Irish* Catholic. That puts a slightly different complexion on things with shades of that 1923 Church of Scotland report still extant. Nobody, however, pointed this out at the time or since, but it gets to the very heart of what the bigotry in Scotland has been, and still is all about.

I have to admit that my own conclusions about the bigotry in Scotland have always been that it is of a sectarian nature. My book *Up to Our Knees* outlined this anti-Catholicism in Scotland. It is permitted, though, to change one's mind and my mind has certainly been changed.

Arthur Wellesley, Duke of Wellington, is one of England's and Britain's great military heroes. He defeated the mighty Napoleon on the battlefield and saved Europe from being under the dominance of the French Emperor. It usually comes as a surprise when folk discover that this quintessential Englishman was, actually, Irish. Then again, in many ways he was not.

The term *Anglo-Irish* was not used until the late 19th and early 20th Centuries to describe those that constituted the Protestant Ascendancy in Ireland. It was used retrospectively as well so that Wellington, to historians, was, and is, referred to as *Anglo-Irish*. This of course, means that he is not considered to be *Irish*. God forbid that should happen!

The Anglo-Irish were, almost exclusively, members of the Anglican Church of Ireland. They could be descendants of the

Normans that settled in Ireland and later became Anglicans; they could be descendants of the Elizabethan English conquerors and they could even be Catholics that had converted to the Church of Ireland. As historian Thomas Flanagan said, 'there were many ways of being Anglo-Irish'.[4]

Meanwhile, the mostly Presbyterian Protestants of Ulster became known as the *Ulster-Scots*. They still call themselves by this name and are referred to as such in the media. This means that they are considered to be entirely separate from the Catholic *Irish* in Northern Ireland. In fact, it is clear that the names *Anglo-Irish* and *Ulster-Scots* imply that these people are *British*, not *Irish*. (All they need is *Welsh-Irish* for the set.)

Since anybody that came from the island of Ireland that happened to be Protestant was considered British, the only *real* Irish were those that were Roman Catholics. The special care that was given to separating these 'British' Protestants from the Irish hordes points to one thing: the 1923 report was not about sectarian hatred; it was anti-Irish racism.

There are those that deny that such racism can possibly exist. Bill McMurdo, for example, on his old blog, argued that anti-Irish racism was an invention of those that wanted to play the victim.[5] If that was really the case, however, then why would anybody go to all the trouble of making sure that certain parties are not considered part of the Irish race? Did those signs saying, 'No dogs, no blacks, no Irish' refer to the Anglo-Irish and Ulster-Scots as well?

In order to suit their agenda that all the Irish do is get drunk on Guinness and then look for somebody to punch, some extraordinary lengths are gone to. Anyone that has gone on the tourist trail in Dublin is bound to have visited the *Dublin Writers Museum*, where the city shows off its great literary past and present.[6] Investigate any of these great, Irish writers while on the British side of the Irish Sea and one is in for a shock.

Jonathan Swift[7], Oscar Wilde[8], George Bernard Shaw[9] and Samuel Beckett[10] are all described as being *Anglo-Irish*. Yeats might have chosen to identify himself as Irish, but it is always made plain that he came from an Anglo-Irish background.[11] Even when it comes to Joyce's biography, great play is made of the fact that he got out of Ireland almost as soon as he could and spent most of his life away from the land of his birth.[12] The implication is that he cannot properly be considered *Irish*.

The agenda behind all this is clear: Ireland would be a cultural wasteland if it had not been for the civilising influence of the English/British. Irish intellectualism is constantly demeaned. A shining example of this is the way Ruth Dudley Edwards describes those that took part in the Easter Rising of 1916. She paints them as dreamers and fantasists; individuals that have no connection to the real world, intellectual or otherwise.[13]

When it comes to The People's attitude in this respect, one only has to listen to their songs to understand how they feel. They are constantly 'up to their knees in Fenian blood' and even in their most anodyne songs, like *Follow Follow*, they sing of Dublin as if it is the last place on earth that anyone would want to go to. It is clear to anyone that pays attention that their hatred of the Irish far exceeds their hatred of Catholics in general.

After Rangers signed Mo Johnston in 1989,[14] the club went on to sign quite a lot of Roman Catholics. In fact, it appeared that Catholics had played for Rangers throughout its history, but they had to keep quiet about their religion. One member of The People inadvertently betrayed the real basis of the prejudice at Rangers when he said,

> We never had a no Catholic policy, it was a no fenian bastard policy. There's a big difference.[15]

In fact, Rangers never signed a Catholic from Ireland throughout its whole lifetime; it was left to the new Ibrox club, Neo-Gers, to do that in 2013.[16] As usual, however, there were apologists ready to claim that Jon Daly was not the first Irish player at Ibrox.[17] The problem was that not one of the players listed at this website was a Catholic. That being the case, it is doubtful whether those Irishmen were considered Irish at all. They were probably, at the time they signed and played for Rangers, looked upon as *Anglo-Irish*.

As for the signing of Jon Daly, not everyone among The People was happy, or even indifferent.

> John Daly? the fucking name gives the game away.
> Has he got a good left foot?

> Fuck off Daly[18]

> Seriously, I've never sang a song at a game before that could have got us into trouble, I've not missed a home game for years and I'm telling you that he should be absolutely nowhere near our club, regardless of football ability, he is a republican bastard who can fuck right off.[19]

> NO NO NO!
> I don't want no scum bag playing for Rangers![20]

As mentioned above, the media in Scotland have always stayed quiet about the country's dirty, little secret. There is the odd mention of the disgusting singing and chanting of The People but, mostly, The People's anti-Irish racism and consequent anti-Catholic bigotry is simply ignored. And yet, when an Ibrox club breaks with tradition the media are suddenly all over it, as if it is a wonderful achievement.

The signing of Mo Johnston is still hailed as a 'momentous' event in Scottish football, with the Daily Record, at the time, gushing about 'how much courage Rangers needed to lance the boil of their notorious sectarian record.'[21] It was strange how that 'notorious sectarian record' was ignored by the Daily Record for all those years.

It was the same when Neo-Gers signed Jon Daly. As the Scotsman put it,

> You can argue that it's sad to still be talking about religion when Rangers (sic) sign a player or you can congratulate them for being responsible enough to break the mould.[22]

In other words, anyone mentioning the inherent bigotry at Ibrox is the one with the problem. We should all be falling over ourselves to pat Neo-Gers on the back for doing something that other folk and other football clubs see as normal.

It is rather telling that nobody wants to face up to anti-Irish racism; instead preferring to call it sectarian bigotry. In this way, they can claim that the bigotry is a two-way street. *Nil By Mouth*, for example, are always keen to balance things, as they see it, by claiming that Catholic schools are centres of sectarian bigotry, which discriminate against Protestant employees.[23] The media, too, are always ready to provide 'balance' and cannot say anything against The People without dragging Celtic and its supporters into things.

The reason why everyone is so reluctant to face up to the problem of anti-Irish racism is because it is not just a 'People' thing or even a 'West-of-Scotland' thing. The truth is that anti-Irish racism is endemic throughout Scotland. Nobody wants to tackle their own racism and anti-Irish racism is the last acceptable bigotry in Scotland.

All over the world, people of Irish descent celebrate their heritage on St. Patrick's Day. Parades and parties are the order of the day and those that are not of Irish descent pretend that they are or just join in anyway.[24] In the UK, the day is a public holiday in Northern Ireland, where there are different festivities, while in England there are festivals and parades in Liverpool, Birmingham and London.[25] In Scotland, however, celebrating Irish heritage has not been encouraged.

In fact, in 2015, Glasgow Council allowed a parade by a crowd of bigots, called *Regimental Blues*, to march down the Gallowgate on the Saturday before St. Patrick's Day.[26] To those unfamiliar with Glasgow, this street contains several 'Celtic' pubs. On the day of the march Celtic were taking on Dundee United in the League Cup Final at Hampden, so those pubs would have been full. It seemed that Glasgow Council just did not care.

This came just a matter of weeks after suggestions that Glasgow should host a St. Patrick's Day parade were shouted down as being 'divisive'. A Labour MP and a Conservative one claimed that the Irish were not an 'ethnic minority' and that celebrating St. Patrick's Day was 'living in the past'.[27] Strangely, neither MP had anything to say about Orange Walks.

Eventually, Glasgow, rather embarrassedly, lit up a few buildings green, which was nothing more than a token gesture. Both Glasgow[28] and Edinburgh[29] now boast about St. Patrick's Day 'events', although it is notable that they all seem to take place in 'Irish' pubs. And while police officers were taking part in parades in Boston and New York, police officers in Scotland warned people not to drink and drive on St. Patrick's Day.[30] Such advice has never been given to the Orange hordes lying pissed in Glasgow Green every July. Obviously, the police do not think they need any such warning; those Irish, on the other hand, everyone knows what they are like…

Up until fairly recently, anti-Irish racism was acceptable throughout the UK. In the 1980s the *Black and White Minstrel Show* was long gone and comedians, like Bernard Manning, who told jokes about black people, were banned from television. Jokes that began, 'Pat and Mick…' and pointed out how stupid Irish people were, however, were still acceptable. Jimmy Cricket would appear with his gormless grin and wellington boots marked 'L' and 'R' to play up to the stereotype, while Irishmen that were fond of a drink were a mainstay in sitcoms. As the 80s came to a close, though, such references to stupid, drunken, violent Irishmen became less prevalent.

Irish people themselves were sick of the way they were being stereotyped and the *Pogues* almost fell foul of this backlash. Ireland was not sure how to react to the band and many objected to their antics and Shane McGowan's frequent drunkenness. Luckily, the band members had their punk backgrounds to ensure them an audience and Shane McGowan's song writing won over many erstwhile critics.

The offensive stereotypes might have disappeared from our television screens (though they can sometimes still be espied – the TV programme *Jack Taylor* or the movie *Grabbers*, anyone?) but bigotry against the Irish is still with us. It might not be the force it once was in England, but in Scotland it is practically an institution. And it is not just about making jokes; it is a deep-rooted fear and hatred that drives it.

The Church of Scotland might have apologised for its pronouncements of 1923 but, in many respects, it was far too late; the damage had been done. If you read some of the pronouncements of The People, you cannot but help sense the echoes of 1923.

> Almost every organisation in the west of scotland is over run with Catholics and people of Irish decent (sic).[31]

> They run the city via the GCC, they infest the ruling political party, they have their own state funded

schools, their chapels - what else is it, exactly, that they want?[32]

Look at those words 'overrun' and 'infest'; they come straight from that report of 1923. They are talking of people as if they are a disease; a plague. It is exactly the same kind of language that was used in Nazi Germany when talking about the Jews. Most folk, however, look the other way and pretend that it does not exist. Journalist Kevin McKenna, in the Guardian, summed up the general view.

> (It is) my view that anti-Irishness in modern Scotland can be prone to exaggeration and can lead to an unfortunate victim complex among those who claim to observe it lurking in the shadows of Scottish society.[33]

He goes even further, employing a well-worn tactic:

> And yet I wonder how Rosa Parks and Martin Luther King would have regarded ordeal by the singing of a dodgy song (*The Famine Song*), they whose people had to endure lynchings, violence and hatred every day of their lives.[34]

This kind of argument is quite often employed by Ruth Dudley Edwards, and other Unionist apologists, to undermine and demean any claims of anti-Irish and anti-Catholic bigotry.[35] Both the suffering of others and the numbers involved are employed to show that the Irish, and those of Irish descent, have nothing to complain about.[36] It is a specious argument, though, since it could be used to diminish the suffering of almost anybody. One could even say that African-Americans had it good compared with the indigenous population of the Belgian Congo. It is a completely ridiculous stance.

In October 2018, a new group, *Call It Out*, was set up to combat anti-Irish and anti-Catholic bigotry. As usual, The People were outraged, as can be seen by the comments on the story in the *Evening Times*.[37] The People, as we saw in Chapter 12, like to twist things around to make it seem as if *they* are the ones that are being picked on. This is a standard tactic of racists everywhere.

Back in the 1990s, education departments made attempts to stamp out any racism in their schools and sent guidelines to teachers so that they could avoid inadvertently making racist remarks. The idea was that phrases like 'a black mark' and 'blacken one's name' should not be used, since they reinforced the notion that anything black was bad. The Catholic Church also sent out guidelines, telling teachers not to employ the old-fashioned idea that sin 'blackened' the soul.

The headteacher of the school I was working at twisted things to make it so that we were not allowed to say the word 'black' at all. The blackboard was to be called the 'chalkboard' and, if doing a project about birds, we should ignore the existence of blackbirds. This was not what the guidelines said, and it simply showed the headteacher up as a 'They come over here…' type of racial bigot. None of the staff was that keen on the woman anyway, but this behaviour put the tin hat on things.

I have also encountered nursery teachers and nurses that swear blind that they were told by senior members of the education department not to sing *Baa Baa Black Sheep*. This story was started by *The Sun* and was proven to be a load of rubbish at the end of the 1980s, but these nursery staff maintained that it was true. Not surprisingly, none of them were able to show any letters they had received regarding this nonsense. Apparently, the Director of Education went round every nursery under his jurisdiction to tell them all personally that the song was banned!

As we have already seen, The People use the same tactics when anybody complains about bigotry. Their favourite tactic is to accuse the ones complaining of being bigots themselves. This message comes through loud and clear in the comments on that *Evening Times* article. To support this agenda, a rather disingenuous argument was brought into the mix.

> Does this apply to Northern Irish protestants or is it only certain Irish people that matter(?)[38]

Now, that was a new angle. Suddenly, Northern-Irish Protestants are to be considered *Irish*, instead of as Ulster-Scots! It is doubtful that your average DUP-supporting, Loyalist Orangeman would thank that individual for describing them as Irish. Surely a card-carrying member of The People should know better than that. The same applies to attempts to argue that the Orange Order is an *Irish* organisation.

> The Orange Order was founded in Ireland and imported here by Irish people.[39]

Oh, dear. So, the Orange Order was imported to Scotland by Irish people? Not according to the Orange Order's own history, which states that Scottish soldiers brought it to these shores from Ulster.[40] And there is that argument again that Ulster Protestants were, and are, Irish. What happened to the Ulster-Scots, the Cruthins[41] and all that?

Another ridiculous argument is that there is no such thing as an 'Irish community' in Glasgow or anywhere else in Scotland. Actually, nobody made any such claim; all they have said is that folk of Irish descent in Scotland face racial discrimination and abuse. Strangely, though, the same ones that say there is no such thing as an 'Irish community' also go on (and on) about something called the 'PUL (Protestant Unionist Loyalist) Community'. They cannot have it both ways but, according to their twisted logic, they can.

They also take great delight in pointing out that the Irish are not a race. Fair enough. But, then, they are perfectly happy to 'call out', as they see it, anti-British and anti-Scottish racism.

> How about these useless khants making statements and condemning the endemic anti-British racism in Scotland?[42]

> It's anti-Scottish racism. Lennon and his supporters are tarring all Scottish people with the racist brush.[43]

The People are also great believers in the myth that those wishing for an independent Scotland are guilty of anti-English racism. So, the English, the Scots and even the British can be considered 'races' but the Irish cannot? As usual, The People trip themselves up with their own arguments.

The big problem with The People is that they just cannot help themselves and revert to anti-Irish racism, even while they claim that no such thing exists and, if it does, nobody is guilty of it.

Has anyone told them that production of Solanum Tuberosum is at levels comparable to that of pre mid-1800's quantities?[44]

A Bear MUST GO TO THIS EVENT (the inaugural meeting of *Call It Out*), UNDERCOVER. Are you capable to fly under a false flag behind enemy lines? Are you brave enough with a strong constitution and a poor sense of smell?[45]

There was a delightful little coda to all this outrage over *Call It Out*. While The People whined and squealed about anti-Irish and anti-Catholic bigotry not existing and there being no need for this new organisation, the inaugural meeting of *Call It Out* had to move to different premises. It was originally scheduled to take place at the Renfield Centre, which is attached to Renfield St. Stephen's Church, a Church of Scotland parish. The meeting had to be cancelled, however, when staff at the Centre received a deluge of threatening phone calls![46]

'A second home for the Irish,' they say.[47] They must be joking!

13
With A Little Help From My Friends

Radio phone-ins about football are a magnet for all manner of bams and conspiracy theorists. The presenters generally argue against whatever the caller is saying and, quite often, the caller will get abusive and start swearing. That is when the caller finds himself getting cut off. Some folk record these mad conversations and put them on social media for everybody to laugh at. One thing that never happens, though, is that such nonsense is considered worthy of making it into the papers.

In December 2018, however, the Daily Record thought that somebody calling in to Radio Clyde's *Superscoreboard* was a big news item. The caller was convinced that the referees in Scotland were conspiring to help Neo-Gers win the league and to stop Celtic winning yet another title. The man said that he had written to FIFA, outlining his complaints. The presenter, Hugh Keevins, said, 'I think writing to FIFA and implying that all the Scottish officials have got together to make life difficult for Celtic and give Rangers a helping hand is madness.[1]'

How the hell anyone thought that newsworthy is the real madness. Conversely, there was not much said about the insane paranoia emanating from Ibrox. We saw in Chapter 11 how Neo-Gers made an official complaint against referee Willie Collum, along with their usual statement. They practically accused him of being prejudiced against their club and the SFA reacted accordingly. But nothing about this paranoia was spoken about in the media; apparently, a phone call from one individual on Radio Clyde was more newsworthy.

Even when Gordon Waddell, in the Sunday Mail, was critical of Neo-Gers, it was couched in terms that criticised all teams. It was pretty much a general rant about clubs only complaining about referees when it affected them.[2] Not a word about paranoia and no sniggering about mad conspiracy theories.

This, however, is standard practice when it comes to how the Scottish media have dealt with Rangers and deal with Neo-Gers. Despite The People's assertions that all the Scottish media are against them, the media actually bend over backwards to keep them appeased. We have already seen how excuses galore were made for the disgraceful behaviour of The People in Barcelona and Manchester; that kind of pathetic sucking up has never changed over the years.

On the 2nd December 2018, while Celtic played Aberdeen in the League Cup final, Neo-Gers faced Hearts in a league game at Tynecastle. Neo-Gers won the game with a goal that came from a free-kick at which three players were blatantly offside. Hearts manager, Craig Levein, was, understandably, incensed. It was not only that decision that angered him; he was also blazing about the number of fouls committed by Alfredo Morelos that went unpunished. He said that it was if his team was playing against thirteen men.[3]

That night BBC Scotland catered for Scottish football fans in the way it usually did, by showing *Sportscene* at a time when most decent, God-fearing folk would be in bed. They, of course, discussed what Craig Levein had said but, instead of analysing what Morelos had done in the game, they showed a foul by a Hearts player, saying that he should have been sent off. It was a petty piece of 'whatabootery' that did not reflect at all well on the presenters. Anybody would have thought they were on Neo-Gers' side!

And it is not just the team the media are biased about. As mentioned earlier, they constantly make excuses for The People or do not mention their behaviour at all. When it comes to Celtic supporters, though, the media are all over it. An example is the way the Evening Times reported on Celtic's visit to Munich in October 2017 to play Bayern in the Champions League. Not only did some Celtic supporters chant *Up the RA* at Manchester Airport, but one supporter actually sang *The Broad Black Brimmer*, which the Evening Times helpfully pointed out is a 'pro-IRA' song, on German TV. To put the tin hat on things, Celtic supporters were, apparently, branded 'piglets' in German media for the mess they left behind.[4]

Well, one can hardly excuse the chants at Manchester Airport, but *The Broad Black Brimmer*? Nobody in Germany has probably ever heard of the song and certainly would not be offended by it. The

IRA, especially the early-Twentieth-Century incarnation, are not viewed by the rest of the world as the monsters that many in the UK would like to think. Even in the UK, and probably even in Ireland, there are many that have never heard of the song and would know nothing about it being 'pro-IRA' unless somebody told them.

As for the 'mess' left behind by the Celtic supporters, that story, if you will pardon the pun, is a load of rubbish. As one commenter pointed out:

'Pity you did not mention the fact that the German police pointed out that there were no rubbish receptacles made available as a general security measure.'[5]

Strangely, or perhaps not so, no mention was made whatsoever in the Scottish media of The People singing their usual, bigoted filth when they went to Croatia to play Osijek in a Europa League qualifier in July 2018.[6] And there was worse to come when Osijek came to Glasgow. There were running battles near Ibrox Stadium, during which two Osijek supporters were stabbed. Of course, if you were to read any of the Scottish newspapers you would be left with the impression that the Osijek fans were fighting with each other and The People were not involved.[7] It was probably those pesky Chelsea supporters again!

This kind of thing, though, is par for the course. In November 2018, the police issued pictures of a man they wanted to speak to in connection with an incident that happened at Pittodrie in August. There the man stood, surrounded by blue football tops and blue and white scarves; obviously he was a Neo-Gers supporter. The Daily Record, however, reported that police were 'probing a glass bottle being launched at fans inside Pittodrie Football Stadium'. That made it sound as if the bottle could have come from anywhere. There is no mention at all of the bottle coming from the Neo-Gers support.[8]

And the media does not stop there. All those that The People view as their enemies are adopted as enemies by the Scottish media as well. For example, every single year James McClean, who comes for Derry and plays for the Republic of Ireland national team, refuses to wear a poppy. And every single year he has got to explain why. He plies his trade in England so, really, it has nothing to do with the Scottish media. The People, however, with their poppy mania, hate McClean with a vengeance, so the Scottish media follows suit.[9]

There is never any mention of all the good and charitable works that McClean gets involved in.[10] The media in England do not seem to have any problem showing the good side of James McClean[11]; nor do those in Northern Ireland.[12] The media in Scotland, though, prefer to keep McClean as a hate figure; it keeps The People onside. With this kind of attempt to normalise the twisted beliefs of The People, it was hardly surprising that they idolised Kirk Broadfoot when he was found guilty of bombarding James McClean with sectarian abuse.[13]

Since The People like to point fingers and blame everybody else for their own bigotry, one of their favourite targets has long been the existence of RC schools. It is not so much the schools themselves that are the issue, apparently, but the fact that they are part of the state system. 'Rome on the rates' was the battle cry in the years after WWI and The People have stuck to this line ever since.

As might be expected, the Scottish media take this line as well and like to occasionally wheel out celebrities to make the point for them. Such a one is Lorraine Kelly, who has, for decades, been the face of breakfast television. In 2008, she was in the Evening Times calling for an end to faith schools.

'To split kids up from their pals at five years old only leads to conflict and suspicion. It gives bigots a chance to pollute the minds of impressionable youngsters and until that stops you will never stamp out the scandal of sectarianism and the deep divisions between all religions.'[14]

When Lorraine Kelly's daughter was a child, they lived in a village in Berkshire called Cookham Dean. The village has its own primary school, which gets good reports and has a good reputation.[15] That, obviously, was not good enough for our Lorraine's daughter, though, and the girl was sent to Herries, a fee-paying school, which happened to be in the village as well.[16]

One cannot help but wonder what wee Rosie's pals thought when she went to a different school from the rest of them. Did it not lead to 'conflict and suspicion'? Strangely, Lorraine Kelly sees nothing wrong with splitting up children on account of one child's parents having more money. It seems that she is not as in favour of children all mixing together as she says. Then again, maybe that just applied to the common scum.

When Rosie reached secondary-school age, the family moved to Broughty Ferry, splitting her from the 'loads of pals' she had made at Herries School. This was not for work or anything, since Kelly still worked in London and had to commute back-and-forth from Dundee.[17] So much for her cry, like Helen Lovejoy, from *The Simpsons*, of 'Won't somebody please think of the children?'! Of course, once ensconced in Dundee, Rosie went to another fee-paying school.[18]

Evidently, then, Lorraine Kelly's opposition to faith schools, which, in Scotland, effectively means RC schools, do not stem from any concerns about children being split up or divisiveness in society. So, why should the daughter of a Catholic mother and a Protestant father, who was born in the Gorbals,[19] take the side of The People in this debate?

For those unfamiliar with Glasgow and its districts, the Gorbals, in the 19th Century, was the place where Irish immigrants to Glasgow first settled. When Kelly was born, in 1959, the place was still full of the descendants of those Irish people, though they were soon to be moved to areas like Castlemilk and, like Kelly's family, East Kilbride. Surely somebody that came from the Gorbals would not be a sectarian bigot and would be against RC schools for purely altruistic reasons?

The fact is that Kelly, although born in the Gorbals, was brought up in Bridgeton. She tends to keep that quiet, but it sometimes slips out.[20] Now, that puts quite a different slant on things. Bridgeton (or *Brigton*, as it is usually called) was not just a Protestant area; it was a decidedly *Orange* one. That is where Billy Fullerton and his Billy Boys resided.[21] One cannot help but wonder what types influenced the young Lorraine Kelly in that environment. She would have witnessed the mourners when Fullerton died in 1962 and would no doubt have been apprised of his legendary status in the area. Maybe she even lived '*Up a wee narrow close, Just by Brigton Cross*'![22]

It is quite remarkable how none of these celebrities paraded by the Scottish media ever blame The People or the Orange Order for sectarian bigotry in Scotland. Neither do the papers ever apportion such blame. Amazingly, The People sing intimidating songs outside Catholic churches, attack Catholic clergy and even stab folk for wearing a Celtic scarf; and, yet, they are not to blame for any of this. The victims, themselves, are culpable for having the gall to attend RC schools.

The fact is, however, that there is no such thing as a non-denominational school in Scotland, especially at primary level. The law in Scotland insists that religious education and celebration are compulsory in primary schools. That education and celebration have to be of the Christian variety and schools are obliged to make links with their local church. Essentially, what are called Non-Denominational schools in Scotland are really *Protestant* schools.[23] Unless the law is changed, that will remain the case.

But it is not just the media in Scotland that provide justification and normalisation for The People' hatreds; organisations that are supposed to be watchdogs for sectarian behaviour do so as well. *Nil By Mouth*, for example, also subscribe to the insane theory that RC schools are responsible for much of the sectarian bigotry in Scotland, while ignoring completely the existence of hate-filled Orange Walks.[24]

The Scottish Government, meanwhile, in 2018, set up a working group to investigate, and make recommendations to tackle, sectarian bigotry in Scotland. Apparently, there was no input at all to this committee from those of Irish descent.[25] Considering the fact that such people are usually the victims of racist and sectarian bigotry, it beggared belief that they would be excluded. It looked as if the result would just be the usual, mealy-mouthed attempt to 'balance things out'.

The appearance of the group *Call It Out* had changed the whole debate about bigotry in Scotland, demanding, as it did, that anti-Irish racism be taken seriously. The committee took this issue into account but performed the usual verbal acrobatics to make the victims seem like the perpetrators and vice-versa. Not only did it recommend that anti-Catholic and anti-Irish bigotry be made hate crimes, but *anti-Protestant* and *anti-British* bigotry as well.[26]

Nil By Mouth cite the phrases 'Hun' and 'Orange bastard' as examples of anti-Protestant bigotry,[27] but this is nonsense. The word 'Hun' refers to anyone associated with Rangers or Neo-Gers. Jock Stein, Kenny Dalglish, Danny McGrain and Henrik Larsson are all Celtic legends and Protestants every one of them. They are *not* Huns. Nacho Novo, Lorenzo Amoruso and Jorge Albertz are Catholics and are also, most decidedly, Huns. It is a simple thing to understand and it is completely disingenuous to pretend that the word means anything else.

As for the term 'Orange bastard', if one is going to sing *The Sash* along with *No Pope of Rome* and *The Famine Song* then that individual deserves the epithet completely. It is not anti-Protestant. A Protestant is a person that attends a Protestant church and I certainly have never heard of folk coming out of such a church to be confronted by a crowd shouting, 'Orange bastards,' at them. The phrase is only used against folk that *are* Orange and *Nil By Mouth*, as usual, are talking nonsense.

And what about that committee's claims about anti-British racism? Where the hell did that come from? Really, it is difficult, if not well-nigh impossible, to think of even one instance of that happening. Probably the laziest, and most widespread, form of racism is the use of stereotypes in so-called jokes. We have all heard them: the criminal, drug-taking black, the Pakistani that stinks of curry, the sex-crazed Italian and the lazy, stupid Irishman. There has never been any such thing as a British stereotype for folk to make jokes about. Maybe such a thing exists in foreign countries; then again, it is the arrogant *English* that most foreigners see as a stereotype.

This desperate 'balancing act', trying to equate a non-existent anti-Britishness with the real experience that folk have had with anti-Irishness is just another, pathetic capitulation to The People. Read any of the Neo-Gers forums, FollowFollow etc., and you soon find out what The People consider to be anti-British racism: singing *The Fields of Athenry*, waving an Irish flag and even being seen without a poppy. Is this the kind of thing that working group meant? Well, there is nothing else to go on, so they must be taking all the nonsense The People churn out at face value.

Not only do The People see anything remotely Irish as being anti-British; they view the campaign for Scottish independence in the same, jaundiced manner. In fact, any criticism levelled at the UK Government, in their opinion, is anti-British. It is unimaginable that the Scottish Government would wish to go down that road, but that would leave them with nothing much to class as anti-British racism. If they do decide to follow up on the working group's recommendations it will just end up being another Offensive Behaviour at Football Act.

It would be remarkably easy for the Scottish Government, the police and every other authority to decide that anything Irish should be considered anti-British. After all, even the middle classes in Scotland subscribe to this theory.

In September 2018 a rugby match took place between two fee-paying, Glasgow schools, St. Aloysius College and Glasgow Academy. St. Aloysius won, and a Glasgow Academy parent, who refused to be named, explained what happened next.

'I could only describe the noise coming from the St. Aloysius changing room as bellowing. It seemed to be all about the IRA and other Irish-related things. Parents were clearly upset and it must have been very embarrassing for people who were there to support St. Aloysius.'[28]

What a wee shame, having to put up with those 'Irish-related things'! Apparently, the team was singing *The Fields of Athenry*,[29] which has nothing at all to do with the IRA. It is clearly about Ireland, though, and that seems to have been enough to upset all those poor parents from Kelvinside or wherever. No doubt they would be perfectly happy for all those St. Aloysius pupils to be rounded up and arrested for anti-British racism.

While the media and Scottish society at large made excuses and normalised the beliefs and behaviour of The People, and continue to do so, the Scottish football authorities have always made sure that their club, their church, has had nothing to answer for. The sectarian signing policy of Rangers was completely ignored, while the bigoted singing and chanting of The People has never been questioned, let alone punished. Probably the most damning indictment of the Scottish football authorities came in 2006, when UEFA decided that it could take no action against Rangers for the sectarian singing of its supporters. The reason was that *The Billy Boys* had been sung in Scotland for years with nothing being done about it, with the result that 'this song is now somehow tolerated'.[30]

The SFA and the SPFL continue to ignore the bigoted singing and chanting of The People and have facilitated all the chicanery involving the new club at Ibrox. Ignoring all the cheating that Rangers did, pretending that the new club is 'still Rangers', secretive Five-Way Agreements; the list goes on. They even ignore the fact that Neo-Gers has been flouting all manner of financial fair play regulations and running up huge amounts of debt. And the scandalous behaviour does not end there.

Dave King was found guilty in South Africa of dodging playing millions in tax, which he had to pay back, along with a fine, if he wanted to avoid prison. The Scottish media has spun this as him 'coming to an arrangement', while the SFA decided that he was a fit and proper person to be chairman of Neo-Gers. Maybe this is not quite as scandalous as it first appears; after all, a crook and a crooked club are made for each other. But there was even worse to come.

In November 2018, while in court trying to weasel out of the Takeover Panel's demand that he make an offer for all the Neo-Gers shares held by those outwith his concert party, King made an astonishing admission. He claimed that four shareholders had links to organised crime.[31] Now, a statement like that should have the police crawling all over it and the SFA should have been starting an investigation. But this is Scotland so...nothing.

Over the years, Scottish referees have done their bit to make the path of The People's team an easy one. We have all read the stories about ex-referees, at Rangers functions, having a laugh about how they stopped the 'Fenians' winning. It is all one, big joke; except that it is not. Many examples exist of referees giving a helping hand to Rangers; a dodgy penalty here, a disallowed goal there. Sometimes, they go to extraordinary lengths.

In 2010, referee Dougie McDonald was caught out lying after giving Celtic a penalty and then, suddenly, changing his mind. That was not the only criticism levelled at referees that season. It was reported in newspapers that 80% of Category One referees in Scotland had failed a written test on the rules of football. And Neil Lennon had the gall to question a decision made in a game against Rangers. The referee's answer to all this criticism was to go on strike.[32]

Rather incongruously, Scotland's referees did not react quite so petulantly when they were subjected to a barrage of criticism eight years later. First off, we had Steven Gerrard, the new Neo-Gers manager, moaning about referees and claiming that they had had it in for 'Rangers' for years.[33] Then, we had the unedifying spectacle of Neo-Gers making an official complaint and releasing a statement about Willie Collum. Scotland's referees said absolutely nothing, even though they were being virtually accused of being biased.

And then Craig Levein made his comment about playing against twelve men in that match at Tynecastle. Former referee, Steve Conroy, claimed that criticism of officials was becoming 'more personal'.[34] Strangely, he had nothing to say about the slating of Willie Collum by Neo-Gers. A month earlier, the same individual was calling for 'strict liability' after Neil Lennon was struck by a coin at Tynecastle, the Hearts goalkeeper claimed that a fan punched him, and the two assistant referees were hit with missiles.[35] It was strange that he had not been so outraged when a Neo-Gers supporter hit a linesman with a coin in a match against Livingston.

Then again, maybe there was nothing strange about it. Conroy resigned as a referee in 2012 after being banished to the lower divisions. He had awarded a penalty to a player that video evidence subsequently showed had dived.[36] No prizes for guessing the name of the team that got the penalty! No doubt Conroy wanted strict liability to apply to every Scottish team except one.

With all these organisations, individuals and social groups doing their utmost to make The People appear normal, you would think that would be enough. But no. Yet another mob feels the need to normalise The People's behaviour. That mob is called *Show Racism the Red Card*.

In July 2018, Shay Logan of Aberdeen claimed that Celtic supporters had made racist comments to him after the last game of the season at Celtic Park in May. Nobody else had heard the comments and there was only Logan's word for it that it had happened at all. *Show Racism the Red Card*, however, felt justified in saying, 'We fully support Shay Logan and will be asking the SPFL to investigate any claims of racism reported to the league.'[37]

Fast-forward a few months and Celtic were playing Aberdeen again; this time at Hampden in the League Cup final. Scott Sinclair stepped up to take a penalty and someone, obviously not a Celtic supporter, shouted out a racially-abusive term. A video of this incident appeared online, in which you can easily hear the shout. *Show Racism the Red Card*'s response?

> Show Racism the Red Card Scotland are saddened to see a video that allegedly shows an Aberdeen FC fan racially abuse Celtic's Scott Sinclair just before he

takes a penalty at the weekend's League Cup Final at Hampden Park.[38]

Alleged? That was not what they said about Shay Logan, with not a shred of evidence to back up their claim. Obviously, this shower has it in for Celtic and its supporters but what about The People? What would they say about them?

There is no need to speculate, since an incident (only one of many) happened in July 2018 when Neo-Gers went to Macedonia to play Shkupi in the Europa League qualifiers. A video did the rounds, showing one of The People racially abusing Macedonian children. This video was uploaded and shared by The People themselves; they thought it was funny. So, what did *Show Racism the Red Card* have to say about it?

'Show Racism the Red Card Scotland were shocked to see the film of racist abuse by a so-called 'Rangers (sic) fan' in Macedonia this week and call upon anyone who has any information regarding his identity to contact Police Scotland.'[39]

So, Show *Racism the Red Card* is just another group making excuses for The People. And that is not the only time they have covered up or ignored the behaviour of The People. Various black Celtic players have had monkey noises and gestures made at them by The People, often in full view of television audiences but not a word has been said by *Show Racism the Red Card*. And when it comes to anti-Irish racism, they simply do not want to know. Only one kind of racism counts and only one group of supporters, it seems, are never guilty of it.

'But…but…but…Mark Walters…bananas…'

Aye, whatever.

14
Que Sera Sera

So, what does the future hold for The People? We are well into the 21st Century now and The People still act as if it is the 17th or 18th. The strange thing is, though, that they simply do not realise it. Like any delusional individuals, they believe that it is everybody else that is out of step with reality. There comes a point, though, when reality begins to intrude into any delusion.

We all struggle to understand the details of Brexit; even the politicians dealing with it do not seem to know what they are doing. Soft Brexit, hard Brexit, backstops; most folk have just given up trying to make sense of it. One detail, however, has jumped out at The People and has brought terror to their hearts. It concerns Northern Ireland being treated differently from the rest of the UK and an open border with the Republic of Ireland remaining in force.

This would necessarily mean a customs border between Northern Ireland and Britain since Ireland is still a part of the EU. And this is what frightens The People. With Northern Ireland having closer economic ties with Ireland than with Britain, it would probably eventually lead to a united Ireland. That, of course, is complete anathema to The People.

The hatred of the People toward everything Irish and Catholic has its roots away in the distant past and they do not even understand the reasons for their hatred anymore. They rationalise, citing child abuse in the Catholic Church and Irish terrorism as supposed reasons for their hatred. The truth is, however, that their hatred long predates the revelations about child abuse in the Catholic Church and the very existence of the IRA or even the Fenians. They hate, but they do not know why, so they grasp at any possible excuse they can find.

Ridiculously, they claim not to hate the Irish or anything to do with Ireland. What they profess to hate are those in Scotland that dare to sing an Irish song, wave an Irish flag or otherwise publicly declare their Irish descent. The People call such folk *Plastic Paddies*. Meanwhile, there are groups in Scotland calling themselves the

Apprentice Boys of Derry marching around in sashes and bowler hats. Most of the members do not come from Derry and probably have no links to the place at all. We saw, in Chapter 12, how, to suit their own agenda, The People have taken to calling Protestants form Northern Ireland 'Irish'. Er…does that not mean that all those Scottish Apprentice Boys are *Plastic Paddies*?

In this modern, global age The People get themselves all in a muddle about whom they are supposed to hate. On the 12th July, and the previous evening's *Bonefire* Night, Swastika flags can be seen flying next to those of the old American Confederacy and of Israel. This ridiculous state of affairs comes about simply because they take their cue from their 'enemies'. Irish Nationalists profess anti-racism, which makes The People automatically racist. Irish Nationalists also support the Palestinians, so The People are on the side of Israel. They really are a mixed-up bunch.

These days, younger people have access to much more information that my generation ever had. Social media is worldwide, which means that those in their teens and twenties are used to having instant conversations with people in other countries. They can even play games on the Playstation and X-Box with folk on the other side of the world. They have also grown up in a multi-cultural society, which, obviously, colours their view of the world. This state of affairs means that Loyalist parties in Northern Ireland are steadily losing voters.

There are many young people in Northern Ireland that want to remain part of the UK but have nobody they feel they can vote for. They are sickened by the DUP's sexist, homophobic and even racist policies to the extent that they no longer vote at all. The Loyalist movement is going to have to choose which is more important to it: staying in the UK or all its religiously-inspired policies. It might be a good idea as well to abandon all the stuff about the world being created 4,000 years ago and Jesus riding into Jerusalem on a stegosaurus.

The only possibility of salvation and a future for The People, both in Northern Ireland and in Scotland, lies in their long-standing disdain for intellectualism and even education. Have a look at the ones in their teens and twenties that play in Orange bands or walk at the back among the sky punchers and you can see from their faces that there is not much going on between their ears. Never mind social media; those characters would need help just to plug a computer in.

In the old days, education did not matter at all to The People; good jobs were lined up for them in heavy industry, no matter how thick they were. Looking at the numbskulls among The People these days, it is a wonder that anything got built at all. Those heavy industries have all gone now and even The People are coming to realise that their offspring are going to have to compete for jobs in a shrinking market. They might think it totally unfair but, at the very least, their children are going to have to consent to a basic education.

The problem is, though, that even somebody with a basic education can see how wrongheaded The People are. And that is the dilemma facing The People: encourage their kids to get an education and a decent job but run the risk of losing them to the real world or ensure the continuation of The People by keeping their children perpetually thick. We all know what normal folk would do but 'normal' is not a word that can be associated with The People.

Society has seen massive changes in the first two decades of the 21st Century. Back in 2001, getting on the internet was often more trouble than it was worth. First, you had to make sure that nobody wanted to use the phone or was expecting a call. Then, you had the horrible noise of the dial-up modem, which often took a few attempts to connect. Downloading even a short video could take days, so nobody really bothered. And go to the wrong website and your computer could download a dialler, which, when you next tried to get on the internet, took you straight to some porn site that cost £2 a minute or more. My brother had to fix somebody's computer that had ten diallers on it, all competing to connect and making the operating system crash. Things have changed a lot since then.

Nowadays, most young people connect to the internet using their mobile phones. In fact, they do not 'connect', in the old sense, at all but stay connected all the time. Speeds are so fast that nobody downloads videos anymore; they stream them and moan like hell if there is as much as a two-second delay. You can watch TV programmes or movies on your phone and upload pictures and videos to social media. And social media is what it is all about.

Facebook, Instagram, WhatsApp; they have all had their moment in the sun and then young people have moved on to something else. God alone knows what the trendy social media are at the moment;

as soon as we old fogies discover what it is, young people move onto something else. These sites and apps are not about sharing information; they are all about popularity. All that matters is the number of followers you have and you will do anything to get them. Those followers, though, have to be the right kind of people: folk that have far more followers than you, celebrities, well-known trendsetters etc. Posting 'Fuck the Pope' in capital letters is hardly going to cut it.

So, the offspring of The People have their own choices to make. Do they want to be popular among their peers on social media or do they want to appeal to sad, old tossers with bigotry and racism? If nothing else, their baser instincts will tell them which to choose. They are hardly likely to get a shag off one of those old Huns on Twitter, are they?

Of course, there are still the terminally thick that can see nothing better than wearing the sashes, and probably the socks and underpants, their fathers wore. Social media is beyond such individuals; they are incapable even of making a phone call on one of those mobiles. Their favoured means of communication is a badly-spelt sign painted on a wall or an old bedsheet. They also try to organise visual displays at Ibrox but their inability to use social media means that none of them know what they are supposed to be doing. That is why their *tifos* always end up being complete shambles.

It is these morons that The People are going to have to rely on if their new religion is to keep going. The problem is, those morons will have to be persuaded to breed within their own, small group; other genes might dilute their stupidity. As time goes on, however, this will lead to arrests and even more toes than they have at present. It is not the best way to plan the continuation of the tribe. But, unless great strides are made in producing babies in a factory, like in *Brave New World*, there is not much else they can do.

We saw, in Chapter 10, how the world seems to be moving to the extreme right politically, which should be good news for The People. Unfortunately, although they share the same hatreds as Nazi and fascist groups in Europe and America, they have got themselves into their usual muddle. They have gone on for years about U-boats refuelling on the west coast of Ireland and lights being left on down the east coast to guide the Luftwaffe in. Essentially, they have made out that the Irish were Nazis, while fascism was a Catholic thing, burgeoning as it did in Spain and Italy. It is difficult to square those beliefs with support for modern-day fascists and Nazis. Somehow, though, they manage it, while denying that they have any connections with such groups.

Holding onto two opposing beliefs is called *cognitive dissonance* and can lead to some serious psychological disorders. The People avoid these disorders mainly due to their lack of brainpower. For centuries, they have been taught to believe that they are always right; every other thought is subordinate to this. They can express fascist and Nazi beliefs but deny that they do; they honestly believe that they are incapable of being fascists or Nazis. Being thick can sometimes be a blessing. They never feel conflicted because they do not understand the things they believe; they simply believe what they are told to believe. It is one of those occasions when ignorance is obviously bliss.

Outside of the political arena, of course, is the club. But even that is often not enough to keep The People going; they are notoriously fickle, after all. Those of us old enough to remember the first half of the 1980s, when John Greig and Jock Wallace were in charge, can easily recall the small crowds and vast, open spaces among the terraces. Rangers were not winning much, so The People all but deserted them.

Things could easily go the same way in the near future; there are only so many times you can claim to be 'going for 55'. Every year, it seems, a new Messiah turns up at Ibrox, just like Jock Wallace in 1983, and it always ends up the same way. There will eventually come a time when they are going to ask themselves what the point is. That might well come sooner rather than later, and it will be their own fault.

Whenever Neo-Gers lose, or even draw, The People have become accustomed to blaming the referee and other officials. They are even calling for VAR, as was used in the 2018 World Cup, to be introduced into Scottish football. Of course, this is a knee-jerk reaction from The People and, deep down, they probably hope that nobody in authority is listening. If VAR were to be introduced, and used properly, then they know, as well as everyone else, that their team would soon be floundering about at the bottom of the table.

There are characters on FollowFollow and other forums that keep a list of all the decisions that go against Neo-Gers and all those in their favour. The problem is that they do not see anything wrong with many of the decisions that *do* go in their favour. If an opposition player gets sent off, they view it as the correct decision, no matter what the circumstances. If a linesman incorrectly flags one of their players offside, then that goes straight into the 'against' column. If one of their players, however, was offside but the goal is allowed to stand, that does not go in the 'for' column. In their opinion it was a legitimate goal, and everybody is lying about the player being offside. This, rather obviously, means that the 'against' column is a lot bigger than the 'for'.

In reality, Neo-Gers rely on the officials for most of their victories. If that help were to be compromised in any way, for example, if VAR started to be used, the truth is that Neo-Gers would win very few games. As they drifted down the league table, so The People would drift away from Ibrox. Eventually, there might well be no Neo-Gers supporters left at all. And that is not the only danger.

Since its inception, Neo-Gers has been running up debts to keep going. This way of operating is unsustainable in the long term and was one of the reasons for the death of the old club. Unless the club starts to win some major prize money, or an unlikely benefactor with bottomless pockets appears, it is just going to go the same way as its predecessor. All the dodgy shenanigans that occurred with the liquidation of Rangers, though, might not be allowed to happen with Neo-Gers.

Despite assurances from Dave King, Mike Ashley and Sports Direct have been haunting Neo-Gers for years now. Just when the media announces that he has gone for good, up he pops again, bleeding more money out of the club. If liquidation *were* to happen, then Ashley would make sure it was a proper one. There would be no backstairs deals with the likes of Green.

That, however, is an unlikely scenario. The Scottish Establishment relies on these forelock-tugging knuckle-draggers to stay in power, so a 'Rangers' of some kind will probably always exist. Not only that, but a helping hand will always be extended, both by officials in the game and a blind eye being turned to any financial irregularities. There is, however, a downside to all this as far as The People are concerned.

Imagine if all the dreams of The People were to come true. Imagine Celtic went out of business, Celtic Park was flattened, and the club simply ceased to exist. Then, some fascist government came to power that forced all of us of Irish descent to 'go home'. The Catholic Church is then completely banned, with anyone disobeying the law imprisoned or even put to death. And 'Rangers' would be government-funded, and all the stops pulled out to make sure they won everything in Scotland and were a force to reckon with in Europe. The People would believe that the Millennium had come at last.

The problem is, however, that The People, for centuries, have been taught nothing but hatred. If there is nobody left for them to hate, then where are they going to direct it? It would be back to square one, with the Scottish Establishment, as it was four-hundred years ago, faced with a seething mass of hatred that might well turn on its 'betters'. That is something that cannot be allowed to happen.

So, The People might feel secure in the knowledge that the Scottish Establishment is fighting their corner. Unfortunately for them, the Establishment also needs the presence of folk of Irish descent, Catholics and, of course, Celtic Football Club. It is a rather frightening set of circumstances that The People have to face; they cannot be allowed to exist unless their 'enemies' exist as well. Luckily, they are too thick to realise it!

NOTES

INTRODUCTION
[1] http://www.guinnessworldrecords.com/world-records/78669-most-domestic-league-titles

CHAPTER 1
[1] Matthew 16:19 King James Bible
[2] https://www.history.com/topics/martin-luther-and-the-95-theses#
[3] https://www.nationalgallery.org.uk/paintings/jan-van-eyck-the-arnolfini-portrait
[4] https://www.thoughtco.com/renaissance-humanism-p2-1221781
[5] http://shakespeare-online.com/quickquotes/quickquotepiecework.html
[6] http://historyguide.org/intellect/humanism.html
[7] https://www.christianitytoday.com/history/people/theologians/augustine-of-hippo.html
[8] ibid
[9] https://www.christianforums.com/threads/st-augustine-on-predestination.6562895/
[10] http://www.tecmalta.org/tft192.htm
[11] I Corinthians 14:34 King James Bible
[12] I Corinthians 11:14 King James Bible
[13] http://www.ctsfw.net/media/pdfs/reynoldserasmusresponsibleluther.pdf
[14] https://www.britannica.com/event/Peasants-War
[15] http://zimmer.csufresno.edu/~mariterel/against_the_robbing_and_murderin.htm
[16] http://www.theologian-theology.com/theologians/john-calvin-predestination/
[17] ibid
[18] ibid
[19] Matthew 19:24 King James Bible
[20] https://en.wikipedia.org/wiki/Erasmus#Disagreement_with_Luther
[21] http://germanhistorydocs.ghi-dc.org/sub_image.cfm?image_id=3321
[22] https://en.wikipedia.org/wiki/Erasmus#Disagreement_with_Luther
[23] Genesis 17:11–12 King James Bible

CHAPTER 2
[1] Bygone Punishments in Scotland PDF at https://iluminatidiscoroadshow.wordpress.com/2018/07/19/pdf-documents-for-the-people/
[2] https://en.wikipedia.org/wiki/Christmas_in_Scotland
[3] https://www.historic-uk.com/HistoryUK/HistoryofScotland/The-Auld-Alliance-France-Scotland/
[4] https://en.wikipedia.org/wiki/Church_Patronage_(Scotland)_Act_1711
[5] Bygone Punishments in Scotland PDF pp297-298 at https://iluminatidiscoroadshow.wordpress.com/2018/07/19/pdf-documents-for-the-people/
[6] https://www.ed.ac.uk/education/about-us/maps-estates-history/history/part-one
[7] http://www.conservapedia.com/Church_of_Scotland
[8] http://www.rpcscotland.org/shorter-catechism/
[9] http://www.staloysius.rcglasgow.org.uk/stjohnogilvie

[10] https://www.undiscoveredscotland.co.uk/usbiography/g/jennygeddes.html
[11] http://www.covenanter.org.uk/whowere.html
[12] http://www.scotlandmag.com/magazine/issue49/12009599.html
[13] http://jacobite.ca/documents/16870404.htm
[14] https://www.parliament.uk/about/living-heritage/evolutionofparliament/parliamentaryauthority/revolution/collections1/collections-glorious-revolution/billofrights/
[15] http://struggle.ws/talks/king_billy.html
[16] http://www.ulsterancestry.com/ulster-scots.html

CHAPTER 3

[1] http://scottish-history.com/clearances.shtml
[2] http://scottish-history.com/clearances2.shtml
[3] ibid
[4] https://www.historyireland.com/18th-19th-century-history/the-men-of-no-popery-the-origins-of-the-orange-order/
[5] ibid
[6] https://ipfs.io/ipfs/QmXoypizjW3WknFiJnKLwHCnL72vedxjQkDDP1mXWo6uco/wiki/Anti-clericalism.html
[7] https://en.wikipedia.org/wiki/Wolfe_Tone
[8] https://en.wikipedia.org/wiki/Cornelius_Grogan
[9] https://en.wikipedia.org/wiki/Six_Clerks
[10] https://en.wikipedia.org/wiki/Bagenal_Harvey
[11] http://ulster-scots.com/uploads/91262880996.PDF
[12] http://www.nspresbyterian.org/INDEX.HTM
[13] http://brianjohnspencer.blogspot.com/2016/02/from-united-irishmen-to-unionists.html
[14] ibid
[15] http://www.theirishstory.com/2017/10/28/the-1798-rebellion-a-brief-overview/#.W08s1fZFxjp
[16] http://brianjohnspencer.blogspot.com/2016/02/from-united-irishmen-to-unionists.html
[17] http://brianjohnspencer.blogspot.com/2016/02/from-united-irishmen-to-unionists.html
[18] https://www.historyireland.com/18th-19th-century-history/the-men-of-no-popery-the-origins-of-the-orange-order/
[19] http://www.fsmitha.com/h3/h34-ireland.htm
[20] http://brianjohnspencer.blogspot.com/2016/02/from-united-irishmen-to-unionists.html
[21] https://www.historyireland.com/18th-19th-century-history/the-men-of-no-popery-the-origins-of-the-orange-order/
[22] https://en.wikipedia.org/wiki/Croppies_Lie_Down
[23] https://www.historyireland.com/18th-19th-century-history/the-men-of-no-popery-the-origins-of-the-orange-order/
[24] History of The Orange Order PDF at https://iluminatidiscoroadshow.wordpress.com/2018/07/19/pdf-documents-for-the-people/
[25] http://members.pcug.org.au/~ppmay/acts/relief_act_1793.htm
[26] http://ourfightfordemocracy.blogspot.com/p/pitt.html

[27] http://ourfightfordemocracy.blogspot.com/p/pitt.html
[28] https://en.wikipedia.org/wiki/Sydney_Smith
[29] http://www.historyofparliamentonline.org/periods/hanoverians/ultra-tories-and-fall-wellington-government-1830
[30] History of the Orange Order PDF at https://iluminatidiscoroadshow.wordpress.com/2018/07/19/pdf-documents-for-the-people/
[31] ibid
[32] http://scot-buzz.co.uk/stabbed-in-the-back-20-of-the-best-ever-political-put-downs/
[33] http://www.victorianweb.org/history/pms/peel/peel5.html
[34] ibid
[35] History of the Orange Order PDF at https://iluminatidiscoroadshow.wordpress.com/2018/07/19/pdf-documents-for-the-people/
[36] Samuel Green - Scotland 100 Years Ago (Bracken Books, 1994) p 88
[37] http://www.heraldscotland.com/news/13086699.Famine_myth_warning_by_top_historian/
[38] Bygone Punishments in Scotland PDF pp 176-185 at https://iluminatidiscoroadshow.wordpress.com/2018/07/19/pdf-documents-for-the-people/
[39] Religion in Scotland 1840-1940 PDF p2 at https://iluminatidiscoroadshow.wordpress.com/2018/07/19/pdf-documents-for-the-people/
[40] ibid
[41] http://www.sneps.net/OO/images/1-The%20Orange%20Order%20in%20Scotland%20since%201860.pdf
[42] http://www.localhistories.org/ireland19th.html
[43] http://sites.scran.ac.uk/shelf/friend/12.php
[44] https://en.wikipedia.org/wiki/Hope_UK
[45] http://www.sneps.net/OO/images/1-The%20Orange%20Order%20in%20Scotland%20since%201860.pdf p22

CHAPTER 4

[1] Andrew Sanders, Scottish Football and Sectarianism PDF, p5 at https://iluminatidiscoroadshow.wordpress.com/2018/07/19/pdf-documents-for-the-people/
[2] 'And If You Know Your History '. An Examination of the Formation of Football Clubs in Scotland and their Role in the Construction of Social Identity PDF p101 at https://iluminatidiscoroadshow.wordpress.com/2018/07/19/pdf-documents-for-the-people/
[3] ibid
[4] Ibid p98
[5] http://www.glasgowwestaddress.co.uk/1909_Glasgow_Men/Primrose_Sir_John_Ure.htm
[6] https://theninthwavenovel.wordpress.com/2013/05/29/souperism-and-the-politics-of-aid-2/
[7] https://www.bbc.co.uk/news/world-europe-44898434
[8] 'And If You Know Your History '. An Examination of the Formation of Football Clubs in Scotland and their Role in the Construction of Social Identity PDF p100 at

https://iluminatidiscoroadshow.wordpress.com/2018/07/19/pdf-documents-for-the-people/

[9] ibid p99

[10] Andrew Sanders, Scottish Football and Sectarianism PDF, p9 at https://iluminatidiscoroadshow.wordpress.com/2018/07/19/pdf-documents-for-the-people/

[11] https://www.scotsman.com/sport/football/teams/celtic/the-old-firm-story-when-fans-joined-forces-to-riot-1-4162491

[12] https://prezi.com/ehwlofewuibh/why-did-the-conservatives-lose-the-1906-general-election/

[13] https://en.wikipedia.org/wiki/Elections_in_Scotland#1906

[14] https://en.wikipedia.org/wiki/United_Kingdom_general_election,_1906#/media/File:Ten_Years_of_Toryism.jpg

[15] ibid

[16] https://en.wikipedia.org/wiki/John_Ure_Primrose

[17] Andrew Sanders, Scottish Football and Sectarianism PDF, p10 at https://iluminatidiscoroadshow.wordpress.com/2018/07/19/pdf-documents-for-the-people/

[18] https://en.wikipedia.org/wiki/Lodge_Mother_Kilwinning

[19] https://simonmayers.com/2013/12/28/the-masonic-and-orange-orders-fraternal-twins-or-public-misperception-guest-blog/

[20] ibid See first comment

[21] http://kerrydalestreet.co.uk/topic/499392/1/

[22] Andrew Sanders, Scottish Football and Sectarianism PDF at https://iluminatidiscoroadshow.wordpress.com/2018/07/19/pdf-documents-for-the-people/

CHAPTER 5

[1] https://bleacherreport.com/articles/146983-rangers-fans-not-manufactured-chosen

[2] https://www.gersnet.co.uk/index.php/online-museum/history-articles/508-bill-struth-a-rangers-legend

[3] https://www.telegraph.co.uk/sport/football/teams/rangers/10418966/Rangers-fans-find-cold-comfort-in-tales-of-legend-Bill-Struth.html

[4] https://rangers.co.uk/club/history/hall-of-fame/sam-english/

[5] https://www.telegraph.co.uk/sport/football/teams/rangers/10418966/Rangers-fans-find-cold-comfort-in-tales-of-legend-Bill-Struth.html

[6] Pat Anderson Damned Agnivores: Fear, Fraud and Foreigners Chapter 14

[7] https://web.archive.org/web/20080828121803/http://www.followfollow.com/news/loadfeat.asp?cid=ED31&id=300264

[8] https://en.wikipedia.org/wiki/Bevin_Boys

[9] https://www.thescottishsun.co.uk/sport/football/1393465/rangers-fans-petition-wwii-titles-recognised/

[10] https://ipfs.io/ipfs/QmXoypizjW3WknFiJnKLwHCnL72vedxjQkDDP1mXWo6uco/wiki/1941–42_in_Scottish_football.html

[11] https://rangers.co.uk/club/history/hall-of-fame/willie-waddell/

[12] http://www.rsssf.com/tabless/scotchamp.html

[13] https://www.theguardian.com/sport/blog/2014/sep/04/forgotten-story-rangers-1972-european-cup-winners

[14] ibid

[15] ibid
[16] https://www.thescottishsun.co.uk/sport/football/1052307/rangers-european-cup-winners-cup-replay/
[17] https://www.theguardian.com/football/blog/2008/dec/23/rangers-celtic
[18] ibid
[19] https://www.scotsman.com/sport/football/rae-faces-a-six-game-ban-for-head-kick-1-543322
[20] https://en.wikipedia.org/wiki/1971_Ibrox_disaster#Consequences
[21] ibid
[22] ibid
[23] https://www.therangersstandard.co.uk/index.php/articles/fan-culture/165-ibrox-the-forgotten-disaster
[24] http://blog.woolwicharsenal.co.uk/archives/8417 See the Comments.
[25] https://www.birminghammail.co.uk/sport/football/football-news/aston-villa-glasgow-rangers-violence-11998302
[26] https://www.manchestereveningnews.co.uk/news/greater-manchester-news/gallery/one-manchesters-worst-nights-violence-14668447
[27] http://www.bbc.co.uk/scotland/sportscotland/asportingnation/article/0047/print.shtml
[28] http://speedydeletion.wikia.com/wiki/1972_European_Cup_Winners%27_Cup_Final_riots
[29] https://www.scotsman.com/sport/no-hiding-place-for-the-guilty-1-1433332
[30] ibid
[31] ibid
[32] http://www.skysports.com/football/news/11781/3583962/rangers-escape-uefa-action
[33] http://speedydeletion.wikia.com/wiki/1972_European_Cup_Winners%27_Cup_Final_riots
[34] https://www.scotsman.com/sport/rangers-3-2-moscow-dynamo-rangers-the-dynamos-as-they-take-euro-cup-1-1168074
[35] https://www.scotsman.com/sport/tom-english-looks-back-at-the-1980-scottish-cup-final-riot-between-rangers-and-celtic-fans-and-asks-who-was-to-blame-1-1367411

CHAPTER 6
[1] http://www.lodgepollok.org.uk/772_lodge_history.htm
[2] https://rangers.co.uk/news/headlines/loving-cup-ceremony/
[3] https://www.followfollow.com/forum/threads/loving-cup-anniversary.6348/
[4] ibid
[5] http://forum.rangersmedia.co.uk/topic/317318-croats-kicking-off/
[6] https://www.followfollow.com/forum/threads/police-scotland-glasgow-politicians.39463/
[7] http://www.scotzine.com/2013/01/rangers-remembrance-day-parade-branded-inappropriate/
[8] https://en.wikipedia.org/wiki/Armed_Forces_Day_%28United_Kingdom%29
[9] https://www.armedforcesday.org.uk/about/
[10] https://rangers.co.uk/news/club/armed-forces-day-ibrox/
[11] https://www.armedforcescovenant.gov.uk/about/
[12] https://twitter.com/euan_meechan/status/902904407154675712
[13] https://ensignmessage.com/articles/the-people-of-gods-choice/
[14] ibid

[15] https://www.followfollow.com/forum/threads/bill-mcmurdo-jnr-remember-him.35625/

[16] http://www.aforceforgood.org.uk/vision/5000yrs

[17] http://www.aforceforgood.org.uk/vision/service

[18] https://thewordfrommcmurdo.wordpress.com/

[19] https://www.belfasttelegraph.co.uk/opinion/news-analysis/rangers-and-unionism-its-a-question-of-identity-30451365.html

[20] http://www.bbc.co.uk/religion/religions/rastafari/

CHAPTER 7

[1] http://www.sneps.net/about-me

[2] http://www.sneps.net/

[3] The Orange Order in Scotland since 1860 PDF p.3 at https://iluminatidiscoroadshow.wordpress.com/2018/07/19/pdf-documents-for-the-people/

[4] http://lyrics.wikia.com/wiki/The_Thornlie_Boys:No_Pope_Of_Rome

[5] http://www.churchofscotland.org.uk/connect/ecumenism

[6] http://nunraw.blogspot.com/2009/01/earl-lauderdale-pilgrimages.html

[7] The Orange Order in Scotland since 1860 PDF pp.20-21 at https://iluminatidiscoroadshow.wordpress.com/2018/07/19/pdf-documents-for-the-people/

[8] http://www.churchofscotland.org.uk/about_us/our_faith/statements_of_the_churchs_faith

[9] https://freechurch.org/about/beliefs

[10] https://www.theguardian.com/world/2017/jun/08/scottish-episcopal-church-votes-to-allow-same-sex-weddings

[11] https://www.theguardian.com/uk-news/2017/may/25/church-of-scotland-step-towards-conducting-same-sex-marriage

[12] http://ship-of-fools.com/mystery/uk.html

[13] https://www.belfasttelegraph.co.uk/news/northern-ireland/satanic-islam-sermon-belfast-pastor-james-mcconnell-says-he-faces-six-months-in-jail-31313817.html

[14] http://www.glasgowhistory.co.uk/Other%20Sections/100%20Churches/GlasgowEvanChu.htm

[15] ibid

[16] ibid

[17] The Orange Order in Scotland since 1860 PDF at https://iluminatidiscoroadshow.wordpress.com/2018/07/19/pdf-documents-for-the-people/

[18] ibid pp.32-34

[19] ibid

[20] Pat Anderson Up to our Knees; Anti-Catholic Bigotry in Scotland Chapter 6 (pp. 36-37)

[21] https://www.historyireland.com/18th-19th-century-history/the-scottish-irish-orange-connection/

[22] ibid

[23] https://www.vanguardbears.co.uk/

[24] https://www.vanguardbears.co.uk/about/

[25] https://www.vanguardbears.co.uk/article.php?i=185&a=cultural-celebrations

CHAPTER 8
[1] https://www.tatler.com/article/the-future-of-scotland
[2] https://www.vanguardbears.co.uk/article.php?i=185&a=cultural-celebrations
[3] http://islamversuseurope.blogspot.com/2011/10/muslims-demand-suppression-of.html
[4] ibid
[5] http://www.irishnews.com/news/2016/07/11/news/paramilitary-and-racist-displays-put-on-loyalist-bonfire-599868/
[6] http://www.dailymail.co.uk/news/article-4687042/Police-probe-racist-Sinclair-banner-Belfast-Bonfire.html
[7] Connal Parr Inventing the Myth: Political Passions and the Ulster Protestant Imagination Intoduction
[8] https://www.rte.ie/archives/2018/0117/933975-belfast-slum-clearance/
[9] http://www.bbc.co.uk/history/topics/troubles_everyday_life
[10] https://www.belfasttelegraph.co.uk/opinion/columnists/nelson-mccausland/talk-of-equality-is-meaningless-when-protestant-culture-is-ignored-or-excluded-from-so-many-schools-35658217.html
[11] https://www.belfasttelegraph.co.uk/opinion/columnists/the-ulster-protestant-boasts-so-many-more-shades-than-simply-red-white-and-blue-31015697.html
[12] http://www.bbc.co.uk/history/topics/troubles_everyday_life
[13] Anthony D Buckley – AMITY AND ENMITY: VARIETY IN ULSTER PROTESTANT CULTURE PDF pp6-7 at https://iluminatidiscoroadshow.wordpress.com/2018/07/19/pdf-documents-for-the-people/
[14] http://www.saintsandsceptics.org/collapsing-churches-in-northern-ireland/
[15] https://www.theguardian.com/uk-news/2014/mar/22/anna-lo-racist-abuse
[16] http://www.onreligion.co.uk/religion-culture-or-a-bit-of-both-the-case-of-northern-irish-protestants/
[17] ibid
[18] https://www.independent.co.uk/news/informer-exposes-neo-nazi-football-gangs-tim-hepple-who-infiltrated-the-british-national-party-after-1459707.html
[19] https://www.irishtimes.com/opinion/paisley-s-exclusivist-nationalism-lives-on-in-trump-and-brexit-1.3640962
[20] https://www.washingtonpost.com/news/acts-of-faith/wp/2017/08/14/jews-will-not-replace-us-why-white-supremacists-go-after-jews/?utm_term=.95efa86ffe11
[21] https://www.theguardian.com/football/2007/feb/22/newsstory.sport

CHAPTER 9
[1] https://christianhistoryinstitute.org/magazine/article/women-in-the-early-church/
[2] https://www.livinglutheran.org/2015/09/women-reformation-now/
[3] http://www.swrb.com/newslett/actualNLs/firblast.htm
[4] http://www.theweek.co.uk/politics/19075/new-trend-beards-raises-awkward-questions
[5] ibid
[6] http://www.bible-facts.info/articles/beard.htm
[7] https://www.gresham.ac.uk/lectures-and-events/the-victorians-life-and-death
[8] https://www.history.ac.uk/ihr/Focus/Victorians/szret3.html
[9] http://www.victorianweb.org/economics/wages2.html
[10] https://www.psychologytoday.com/us/blog/all-about-sex/201303/hysteria-and-the-strange-history-vibrators

[11] https://www.historyanswers.co.uk/people-politics/anti-suffrage-the-british-women-who-didnt-want-the-vote/
[12] https://www.historyireland.com/20th-century-contemporary-history/irish-suffragettes-at-the-time-of-the-home-rule-crisis/
[13] https://www.belfasttelegraph.co.uk/opinion/news-analysis/ulster-covenant-womens-signature-role-in-the-fight-against-home-rule-28866873.html
[14] https://www.historyireland.com/20th-century-contemporary-history/irish-suffragettes-at-the-time-of-the-home-rule-crisis/
[15] https://www.rs21.org.uk/2015/06/12/1915-glasgow-rent-strike-how-workers-fought-and-won-over-housing/
[16] https://remembermarybarbour.wordpress.com/about-mary-barbour/comment-page-1/
[17] ibid
[18] https://www.bl.uk/votes-for-women/articles/the-anti-suffrage-movement
[19] ibid
[20] http://journals.chapman.edu/ojs/index.php/VocesNovae/article/view/329/721
[21] http://www.1917.org.uk/articles/women-in-the-russian-revolution-1917/
[22] http://easter1916.ie/index.php/people/women/
[23] https://en.wikipedia.org/wiki/Agnes_Hardie
[24] https://en.wikipedia.org/wiki/Constituency_election_results_in_the_United_Kingdom_general_election,_1929#Scotland
[25] ibid
[26] https://thebrokenelbow.com/2016/04/08/the-experience-of-women-in-the-ira-and-uvf/
[27] ibid
[28] https://www.4ni.co.uk/northern-ireland-news/89137/condom-survey-reveals-ni-attitudes
[29] https://www.belfasttelegraph.co.uk/news/health/northern-ireland-women-ignoring-contraception-30578590.html

CHAPTER 10

[1] https://thegaysay.com/2015/05/24/peter-tatchell-northern-ireland-is-the-most-homophobic-place-in-western-europe/
[2] http://notchesblog.com/2014/09/16/ian-paisley-1926-2014-and-the-save-ulster-from-sodomy-campaign/
[3] https://www.bbc.co.uk/news/uk-northern-ireland-37791366
[4] http://www.bbc.co.uk/newsbeat/article/36531235/government-to-review-12-month-deferral-period-for-gay-men-donating-blood
[5] ibid
[6] https://www.bbc.co.uk/news/uk-northern-ireland-36435858
[7] https://www.belfasttelegraph.co.uk/news/politics/caleb-foundation-the-creationist-bible-group-and-its-web-of-influence-at-stormont-28787760.html
[8] https://www.theguardian.com/uk-news/2017/aug/04/northern-irish-unionist-parties-alienating-young-protestants-study
[9] https://www.irishtimes.com/news/politics/marriage-referendum
[10] https://www.bbc.co.uk/news/world-europe-44256152
[11] https://www.theguardian.com/uk-news/2017/aug/04/northern-irish-unionist-parties-alienating-young-protestants-study
[12] https://www.belfasttelegraph.co.uk/news/uk/irish-will-shoot-each-other-if-they-want-to-says-stanley-johnson-37426857.html

[13] http://www.rangerscharity.org.uk/news/new-supporters-group-for-rangers-from-lgbt-community
[14] http://forum.rangersmedia.co.uk/topic/319232-gers-launch-ibrox-pride/
[15] http://forum.rangersmedia.co.uk/topic/319232-gers-launch-ibrox-pride/?page=2
[16] http://forum.rangersmedia.co.uk/topic/319232-gers-launch-ibrox-pride/?page=3
[17] http://forum.rangersmedia.co.uk/topic/319232-gers-launch-ibrox-pride/?page=4
[18] http://forum.rangersmedia.co.uk/topic/319232-gers-launch-ibrox-pride/?page=6
[19] ibid
[20] ibid
[21] https://www.belfasttelegraph.co.uk/news/general-election-2017/uup-ends-antibrexit-stance-and-sides-with-dup-to-oppose-sinn-fein-35702386.html
[22] https://www.washingtonpost.com/news/worldviews/wp/2016/06/25/the-uncomfortable-question-was-the-brexit-vote-based-on-racism/?utm_term=.324c2c5532a3
[23] https://www.theguardian.com/politics/2016/jun/26/racist-incidents-feared-to-be-linked-to-brexit-result-reported-in-england-and-wales
[24] https://www.independent.co.uk/news/uk/crime/brexit-hate-crimes-racism-eu-referendum-vote-attacks-increase-police-figures-official-a7358866.html
[25] http://www.irishnews.com/news/northernirelandnews/2016/07/13/news/hate-crimes-in-northern-ireland-have-fallen-after-brexit-602716/
[26] https://www.independent.co.uk/news/science/brexit-britain-latest-news-academics-threaten-to-quit-brain-drain-over-racist-xenophobic-eu-a7133316.html
[27] https://www.bbc.com/bitesize/guides/z897pbk/revision/2
[28] https://www.ushmm.org/collections/bibliography/1933-book-burnings
[29] https://www.aaup.org/article/brief-history-anti-intellectualism-american-media#.W_OP3PZ2tjo
[30] https://historynewsnetwork.org/article/168305
[31] https://www.theamericanconservative.com/dreher/trump-elitism-populism/
[32] https://www.theguardian.com/global/commentisfree/2016/aug/25/donald-trump-nigel-farage-nationalism-bigotry-ukip
[33] https://www.newstatesman.com/politics/uk/2016/08/welcome-britain-where-even-anti-elitist-movements-are-led-elites
[34] https://en.wikipedia.org/wiki/Edward_Carson
[35] https://www.belfasttelegraph.co.uk/opinion/columnists/ruth-dudley-edwards/how-republicans-love-to-perpetuate-the-romantic-myth-31119903.html
[36] https://link.springer.com/chapter/10.1057%2F9780230582255_3
[37] http://worldpopulationreview.com/countries/scotland-population/
[38] https://countrydigest.org/population-of-glasgow/
[39] http://forum.rangersmedia.co.uk/topic/302401-rangers-fans-being-snp-supporters/
[40] ibid
[41] http://forum.rangersmedia.co.uk/topic/302401-rangers-fans-being-snp-supporters/?page=2
[42] https://www.followfollow.com/forum/threads/the-snp-and-the-sun-conspire-to-put-fans-lives-at-risk-ahead-of-glasgow-derby.44754/page-3
[43] https://twitter.com/mckean_kenneth/status/1054075970565664768
[44] http://www.bbc.co.uk/history/events/good_friday_agreement
[45] https://www.independent.co.uk/news/uk/politics/arlene-foster-good-friday-agreement-brexit-deal-dup-northern-ireland-a8564551.html

[46] https://www.theguardian.com/politics/2018/nov/14/theresa-mays-brexit-deal-everything-you-need-to-know
[47] https://twitter.com/JFletcherQS/status/1062834397307719681

CHAPTER 11

[1] https://www.poetryfoundation.org/poems/46560/dulce-et-decorum-est
[2] https://www.msn.com/en-gb/news/columnists/for-the-first-time-ever-this-year-i-wont-be-wearing-a-poppy-this-is-why/ar-BBPparE?ocid=spartanntp
[3] https://www.differentspirit.org/articles/second_coming.php
[4] https://www.differentspirit.org/articles/temple_mount.php
[5] Book of Revelation; Chapter 20
[6] Revelation, 19:11; King James Version
[7] https://www.historytoday.com/alastair-lamb/search-prester-john
[8] ibid
[9] http://news.bbc.co.uk/sport1/hi/football/teams/c/celtic/5287664.stm
[10] http://www.scotzine.com/2012/12/fran-sandaza-interview-opens-up-old-wounds-of-sectarianism/
[11] Genesis, 9: 22-25; King James Version
[12] https://thecelticblog.com/2017/04/blogs/nacho-novo-no-one-will-ever-love-you-honestly/
[13] https://www.amazon.co.uk/I-Said-No-Thanks-Autobiography/dp/1845023234
[14] https://www.belfasttelegraph.co.uk/news/northern-ireland/rangers-legend-nacho-novo-celebrates-the-twelfth-in-belfast-34880841.html
[15] https://freechurch.org/about/beliefs
[16] https://theweeflea.com/2015/06/19/how-to-be-a-progressive-affirming-accepting-welcoming-and-biblical-church/
[17] https://www.theguardian.com/world/2013/may/20/church-of-scotland-gay-ministers
[18] https://inews.co.uk/news/church-of-scotland-votes-draft-new-same-sex-marriage-legislation-laws/
[19] https://www.dailyrecord.co.uk/news/scottish-news/cops-hunt-shaven-headed-thug-12884122
[20] https://www.thescottishsun.co.uk/news/2906326/orange-order-glasgow-priest-attacked-new-march-fears-july-21/
[21] https://www.thescottishsun.co.uk/news/2951928/orange-walk-church-priest-attacked-cancelled-glasgow/
[22] https://www.scotsman.com/regions/glasgow-strathclyde/orange-order-cancels-walk-in-dispute-over-route-1-4789225
[23] https://www.thescottishsun.co.uk/news/3111383/orange-order-cancels-march-glasgow-church-priest-attack/
[24] https://www.thescottishsun.co.uk/news/3535375/glasgow-orange-walk-protestant-protest-council-priest-spat-accusations/
[25] ibid
[26] https://footballtaxhavens.wordpress.com/tag/glasgow-city-council/
[27] https://www.eveningtimes.co.uk/news/14218606.BBC_launch_fresh_Ibrox_boycott_as_Rangers_ban_sports_reporter/
[28] https://www.followfollow.com/forum/threads/radio-scotland-a-big-turn-off.18958/page-2
[29] ibid
[30] https://www.bbc.co.uk/sport/football/46380763

[31] ibid
[32] https://vanguardbears518692592.wordpress.com/2018/03/14/the-anti-rangers-snp/
[33] https://www.dailyrecord.co.uk/sport/football/bomber-brown-nails-his-colours-to-the-mast-1192539
[34] https://www.thescottishsun.co.uk/sport/football/1351159/ex-rangers-player-melsterland-recalls-the-time-he-got-pulled-up-by-ally-mccoist-for-wearing-a-green-tie-to-training/
[35] https://www.dailyrecord.co.uk/sport/football/football-news/rangers-fan-rage-stars-wear-9770929
[36] https://www.dailyrecord.co.uk/sport/football/football-news/pedro-caixinha-bans-rangers-players-10722482
[37] https://www.dailyrecord.co.uk/sport/football/football-news/lassana-coulibaly-pictured-wearing-green-12892508
[38] http://www.scotzine.com/2017/07/sheffield-pensioner-attacked-for-wearing-macmillan-cancer-support-green/
[39] http://www.talkceltic.net/forums/threads/facts-about-the-huddle-must-read.87121/
[40] https://www.dailyrecord.co.uk/sport/football/football-news/rangers-midfielder-andy-halliday-refuses-10804579
[41] http://forum.rangersmedia.co.uk/topic/309017-andy-halliday-refuses-to-huddle-with-gabala-team-mates/
[42] Ibid

CHAPTER 12
[1] http://www.openhousescotland.co.uk/legacy-notorious-campaign/
[2] https://www.belfasttelegraph.co.uk/imported/kirk-says-sorry-for-antiirish-history-28085137.html
[3] https://www.youtube.com/watch?v=oUXhW3JC9Zw
[4] Quoted in Ellen M. Wolff - "An Anarchy in the Mind and in the Heart": Narrating Anglo-Ireland Chapter 2, Section II
[5] http://paddyontherailway12.blogspot.com/2014/01/xenophobia-homophobia-and-coulrophobia.html
[6] https://www.visitdublin.com/see-do/details/dublin-writers-museum
[7] https://www.britannica.com/biography/Jonathan-Swift
[8] https://irishamerica.com/2015/05/roots-is-oscar-irish/
[9] http://www.open.ac.uk/researchprojects/makingbritain/content/george-bernard-shaw
[10] https://www.britannica.com/biography/Samuel-Beckett
[11] https://www.poets.org/poetsorg/poet/w-b-yeats
[12] https://www.biography.com/people/james-joyce-9358676
[13] https://www.amazon.co.uk/Seven-Legacies-Founding-Fathers-Republic/dp/1780748655
[14] https://www.dailyrecord.co.uk/sport/football/football-news/mo-johnston-signed-rangers-how-11839877
[15] http://forum.rangersmedia.co.uk/topic/223051-great-catholic-players/
[16] https://www.dailyrecord.co.uk/sport/football/football-news/ally-mccoist-jon-dalys-signing-1792719
[17] https://www.eire.guide/2015/07/20/the-irish-at-glasgow-rangers/
[18] http://forum.rangersmedia.co.uk/topic/248549-jon-daly/
[19] http://forum.rangersmedia.co.uk/topic/248549-jon-daly/?page=4
[20] http://forum.rangersmedia.co.uk/topic/248549-jon-daly/?page=7

[21] https://www.dailyrecord.co.uk/sport/football/football-news/mo-johnston-signed-rangers-how-11839877
[22] https://www.scotsman.com/sport/football/teams/rangers/jon-daly-on-being-an-irish-catholic-rangers-player-1-2944845
[23] Pat Anderson - Up to Our Knees: ANTI-CATHOLIC BIGOTRY IN SCOTLAND Chapter 9
[24] https://www.history.com/topics/st-patricks-day/history-of-st-patricks-day-parades-around-the-world
[25] https://www.timeanddate.com/holidays/uk/st-patricks-day
[26] https://athousandflowers.net/2015/03/15/scotlands-shame-loyalist-bigots-hijack-st-patricks-day-in-glasgow/
[27] https://commonspace.scot/articles/487/scottish-politicians-opposition-to-treating-the-irish-as-an-ethnic-minority-in-scotland-challenged
[28] https://www.designmynight.com/glasgow/whats-on/st-patricks-day-in-glasgow
[29] https://www.skiddle.com/cities/edinburgh/stpatricksday.html
[30] http://www.scotland.police.uk/whats-happening/featured-articles/st-patricks-day-drink-driving
[31] https://www.followfollow.com/forum/threads/a-new-anti-catholic-hate-crime-action-group.50925/
[32] https://www.followfollow.com/forum/threads/a-new-anti-catholic-hate-crime-action-group.50925/page-2
[33] https://www.theguardian.com/commentisfree/2014/jan/26/anti-irish-hatred-modern-scotland
[34] ibid
[35] Pat Anderson - Up to Our Knees ANTI-CATHOLIC BIGOTRY IN SCOTLAND Chapter 16
[36] Pat Anderson - Get Over It THE PROBLEM WITH IRISH HISTORY Chapter 1
[37] https://www.eveningtimes.co.uk/news/17187354.glasgow-call-it-out-campaign-hosts-public-meeting/
[38] https://www.followfollow.com/forum/threads/a-new-anti-catholic-hate-crime-action-group.50925/
[39] https://www.eveningtimes.co.uk/news/17187354.glasgow-call-it-out-campaign-hosts-public-meeting/
[40] History of the Orange Order PDF at https://iluminatidiscoroadshow.wordpress.com/2018/07/19/pdf-documents-for-the-people/
[41] http://www.marxmail.org/archives/january99/cockshott.htm
[42] https://www.followfollow.com/forum/threads/pfai-srtrc-on-anti-irish-racism.53665/
[43] https://www.followfollow.com/forum/threads/a-new-anti-catholic-hate-crime-action-group.50925/page-10
[44] https://www.followfollow.com/forum/threads/a-new-anti-catholic-hate-crime-action-group.50925/
[45] https://www.followfollow.com/forum/threads/a-new-anti-catholic-hate-crime-action-group.50925/page-3
[46] http://www.deadlinenews.co.uk/2018/10/24/church-cancels-launch-of-anti-sectarian-campaign-after-threats-to-staff-safety/
[47] https://www.designmynight.com/glasgow/whats-on/st-patricks-day-in-glasgow

CHAPTER 13

[1] https://www.dailyrecord.co.uk/sport/football/football-news/rangers-refs-working-together-phone-13683245
[2] https://www.dailyrecord.co.uk/sport/football/football-news/big-problem-rangers-outrage-willie-13571105
[3] https://www.eveningtimes.co.uk/news/17270845.craig-levein-slams-abysmal-bobby-madden-and-claims-hearts-were-playing-against-13-men-in-rangers-clash/
[4] https://www.eveningtimes.co.uk/news/15607253.Video__Celtic_fan_launches_into_pro_IRA_song_live_on_German_TV_as_supporters_are_branded_PIGLETS_in_local_media/
[5] https://www.eveningtimes.co.uk/news/15610723.Celtic_fans____praised____by_Munich_police__   says_club___despite_German_press_branding_them____piglets___/ Comments section.
[6] https://thecelticstar.com/scotlands-shame-no-nuns-priests-rosary-beads-no-comment/
[7] https://www.eveningtimes.co.uk/news/16396745.ibrox-brawl-two-men-stabbed-in-street-battle-were-osijek-fans/
[8] https://www.dailyrecord.co.uk/news/scottish-news/cops-want-trace-fan-after-13662915
[9] https://www.dailyrecord.co.uk/sport/football/football-news/james-mcclean-new-poppy-snub-9151532
[10] https://twitter.com/m1heavey/status/1069666318620733441
[11] https://www.dailymail.co.uk/sport/sportsnews/article-6458805/James-McClean-pays-homeless-people-stay-Londonderry-hotel.html
[12] https://www.derryjournal.com/news/derry-woman-whose-brother-died-while-homeless-praises-james-mcclean-for-doing-beautiful-thing-1-8729949
[13] http://www.scotzine.com/2015/07/rangers-fan-hero-worship-kirk-broadfoot-after-mcclean-sectarian-abuse/
[14] https://www.eveningtimes.co.uk/news/12853004.Lorraine_in_single_faith_school_plea/
[15] http://www.cookhamdean.org/
[16] https://www.sundaypost.com/in10/lorraine-kelly-the-precious-memories-of-my-daughter-rosie/
[17] https://www.eveningtelegraph.co.uk/fp/lorraine-kelly-ill-always-come-back-dundee-home/
[18] https://www.highschoolofdundee.org.uk/
[19] https://marriedwiki.com/wiki/lorraine-kelly
[20] https://www.eveningtimes.co.uk/news/16279235.tvs-lorraine-kelly-says-its-heartbreaking-to-see-demise-of-glasgow-high-street/
[21] https://www.glasgowlive.co.uk/news/history/street-gangs-brigton-billy-boys-12243020
[22] http://lyrics.wikia.com/wiki/The_Thornlie_Boys:No_Pope_Of_Rome
[23] Pat Anderson - Up to our Knees: ANTI-CATHOLIC BIGOTRY IN SCOTLAND Chapter 9
[24] ibid
[25] http://www.theirishvoice.com/news/no-irish-community-invovlement-in-new-sectarianism-working-group/
[26] https://www.dailyrecord.co.uk/news/crime/holyrood-told-sectarianism-should-classified-13591445
[27] https://nilbymouth.org/history/
[28] https://twitter.com/Heavidor/status/1040136767481864192

[29] ibid
[30] http://news.bbc.co.uk/sport1/hi/football/europe/4907724.stm
[31] https://www.bbc.co.uk/sport/football/46403987
[32] https://www.telegraph.co.uk/sport/football/competitions/scottish-premier/8150178/Scotlands-top-referees-take-historic-vote-to-go-on-strike-after-receiving-a-barrage-of-criticism-this-season.html
[33] https://www.thescottishsun.co.uk/sport/football/3027833/rangers-steven-gerrard-scotland-referees/
[34] https://www.bbc.co.uk/sport/football/46431803
[35] https://www.bbc.co.uk/sport/football/46069911
[36] https://www.bbc.co.uk/sport/football/17398419
[37] https://www.theredcard.org/news/2018/7/10/srtrc-scotland-statement-shay-logan
[38] https://www.theredcard.org/news/2018/12/4/racist-abuse-allegedly-directed-at-celtics-scott-sinclair-by-aberdeen-fc-fan
[39] https://thecelticstar.com/called-rangers-fan-blame-show-racism-red-cards-weak-worded-response-scotlands-shame/

Printed in Great Britain
by Amazon